EDITED BY CHARLES E. COLE

ALTERNATE LIFESTYLES

YOUTH MINISTRY NOTEBOOK VIII

A CROSSROAD BOOK
THE SEABURY PRESS • NEW YORK

ACKNOWLEDGMENTS

Grateful acknowledgment is hereby extended to the following publishers and publications for permission to reprint the articles listed:

Una Sancta—"The Christian Style of Life" by James Gustafson.

The New York Times—"Joe Kelly Has Reached His Boiling Point" by Richard Rogin from *The New York Times Magazine,* June 28, 1970. © 1970 by The New York Times Company. Reprinted by permission.

The Christian Century—"Masculinity and Racism—Breaking Out of the Illusion" by Daniel H. Krichbaum. Copyright 1973 Christian Century Foundation. Reprinted by permission from the January 10, 1973 issue of *The Christian Century.*

The National Observer—"Future Shock in Marriage" by Arthur C. Tennies. Reprinted with permission from *The National Observer,* June 30, 1973, copyright Dow Jones & Company, Inc. 1973.

Random House, Inc.—*Chauvinism! How It Works* by Michael Korda.

The Wall Street Journal—"Powwows and Peyote Help Indians Adjust to Life in the Big City" by Susan Margolies. From *The Wall Street Journal,* June 5, 1973. Reprinted with permission of *The Wall Street Journal* © 1973 Dow Jones & Company, Inc. All Rights Reserved.

The Christian Science Monitor—"Where Have All the Radicals Gone?" by Trudy Rubin. Reprinted by permission from *The Christian Science Monitor,* February 23, 1973. © 1973 The Christian Science Publishing Society. All rights reserved.

The Seabury Press
815 Second Avenue
New York, N.Y. 10017

YOUTH MINISTRY NOTEBOOK VIII was prepared for use in the Christian Churches (Disciples of Christ), the Church of the Brethren, the Episcopal Church, the Presbyterian Church in the U.S., the United Church of Christ, and The United Presbyterian Church in the United States of America.

LIBRARY OF CONGRESS CATALOGING IN PUBLICATION DATA

Cole, Charles, 1935-
    Alternate life styles

    (Youth ministry notebook, 8)
    "A Crossroad book"
    1. Church work with youth.   2. Youth—Religious life.   I. Title.
BV4447.C55   248'.83   73-17892
ISBN 0-8164-5707-7

Contents

Alternate Lifestyles

This book is designed to be used by youth and adults engaged in youth ministry in local congregations and parishes. The assumption is that youth and adults will be planning and working together in order to learn, celebrate, and minister as Christians identifying with the *laos,* the people of God. The book has been prepared with senior high youth—approximately ages 15 to 18—in mind.

The changing nature of youth ministry gives written material a different status from that of several years ago. At one time, printed materials were supposed to tell persons on the local level how to plan programs, or the materials supposedly contained the denomination's point of view on certain religious and moral issues. Laypersons (always called "laymen" then) who used such materials expected to find practical help for their problems. Very often they operated on the assumption that youth were subordinate to adults, and they also often assumed that communication was one way, from church authority to lay, from adult to youth.

Now all that is changed. Young persons are more likely to speak up and to want a share in decision-making. On their side, adults are much less secure in their feeling of being authority figures.

Also, local congregations rightly believe they have something to say about what the church is and what it should be doing.

And youth ministry is less likely to be considered a "program" than it is a ministry. On the inside, this ministry equips Christians for the tasks of witness and service in a world full of injustice and cynicism. But ministry also has a thrust of mission to the outside world.

As a result of these and other changes, printed materials have come to be considered with suspicion if not outright rejection. If youth ministry is concerned with personal relationships or action goals or even spiritual development, of what possible use are these old-fashioned devices known as books and articles?

The term *resource* seems most appropriate here. This book, for example, contains ideas, information, questions, and suggestions for action; and the youth group that would have all these varying points of view and sources of stimulation at its disposal without such a book is a rare group indeed.

In addition, the book has tried to retain some of the best features of religious material. First, the articles have been written and selected for *use* in local churches and not merely for entertainment.

Second, the theme of alternate lifestyles makes the material timely and relevant to laypersons, for whom the meaning is active and present.

Third, these resources support *local* groups and individuals. The users and readers will be members of local congregations in most cases. In all cases they will probably want to select from the material for their particular needs. But the basis for formulating the book as it is arises from a democratic and not an elite idea.

How to Use This Book

Planning

Many groups will want to look ahead for a year or perhaps a few months. Maybe in some cases planning has the unfortunate connotation of filling in a schedule or programs or activities. However, an increasing number of youth ministries conceive planning to be an evaluation of the identity of the group and a corresponding projection of goals and means to accomplish those goals.

The discussion questions at the end of each article should help a group dig into the issues and questions involved in that article. If the session leads to more questions, other activities could be planned to exploit the possibilities. So the articles may sometimes provide the basis for planning several sessions on a particular topic or issue. The "Additional Resources" listed at the end of a given article should also help in planning these additional sessions.

Youth Ministry Notebook VIII can help to stimulate thinking as adults and youth plan for a more effective and meaningful ministry:

"The Christian Style of Life: Problematics of a Good Idea" by James M. Gustafson analyzes the idea of Christian style as such. The article may be slightly academic for many. Yet, with a little work and study, it should yield some results for those trying to understand how the idea of style relates to Christian faith. This article could be read with profit by a small group that wanted to approach the question of alternate lifestyles with real understanding, on the members' part, of the basic concept of style.

"Youth on the Move" by Melanie Turner could be used as a basis for planning trips or sessions to help individuals cope with the practical aspects of traveling.

"Committed for Life: Religious Lifestyles" by Lynne Fitch covers a lot of territory. Almost any local group could read part or all of this article and be stimulated to propose activities and learning events for its own group members.

Educational Settings

Many ministries devote considerable time and energy to growth in attitudes, attempts to increase understanding, and procedures meant to change or reinforce values and actions that express those values. *Youth Ministry Notebook VIII* can be employed in the service of educational goals:

"Marriage and Its Variations" by Patricia de Zutter could be read and discussed by leaders or possibly even an entire group in preparation for panels, symposia, films, or other methods to provide discussion of this important theme in the life of youth.

"Future Shock in Marriage" by Arthur C. Tennies has a slightly different approach from the preceding article and could be used to discuss the changing roles of men and women and the implications for the marriage relationship.

"Young and Gay and Alone" by Michael Austin is an autobiographical statement, written under a pen name, and might be read in a session where attitudes toward homosexuals is the focus or perhaps where the effect of sexuality on lifestyle is the major concern.

"Masculinity and Racism—Breaking Out of the Illusion" by Daniel H. Krichbaum may have a slightly misleading title. The article really tries to help white males, particularly WASPs, understand how to expand their identity in order to avoid some of the destructive aspects of straight, white, male culture. One idea is that different groups within a larger group could read and report on this article in conjunction with the Tennies article and the de Zutter article.

"Chauvinism—The Way It Is in the Office" by Michael Korda would provide good background reading if a group wanted to plan a consciousness raising session on issues raised by the feminist movement. This article, along with "Masculinity and Racism," provides specific suggestions about living style resulting from changes instituted by greater freedom for women.

"Where Have All the Radicals Gone?" by Trudy Rubin provides information on some of the activists of the 1960s and offers a model for how a local group might interview old or young activists in its own community.

"The Young Worker: Challenging the Work Ethic?" raises some questions about the working lifestyle that too many assume belongs only to the older generations. In addition to stimulating the thinking of members of the youth group, the article could help members of a panel or other visiting resource persons prepare for a session on youth and the work ethic.

"Case Study of a Commune" by Charlie Skinner gives a participant's "inside story" of one commune. This study could be used not only to provide information on a possible communal style but to raise questions that might be explored with members of the communes that now seem to be popping up in every area.

Ministry and Mission

Many groups will be more interested in action, not just the single project, but the continuing "doing" to and for the neighbor that arises out of Christian "being." To this end the following resources might be employed:

"Black Consciousness: An Interview with C. Eric Lincoln" provides the views of an outstanding thinker and writer on the subject of black consciousness and the churches. Reading and discussing this article should be helpful to anyone concerned with an activist lifestyle and its relation to Christian faith.

Similarly, "Los Hispanos: A Different Style" by Daniel Alvarez quietly makes a few points about the styles of Spanish-speaking groups in this country and should help those who are seeking action ministries to benefit and involve Chicanos.

"Joe Kelly Has Reached His Boiling Point" by Richard Rogin is intended as background reading for those in the church who want to include either the working person or the so-called ethnics (although perhaps everyone could be called an ethnic) in the scope of Christian ministry. Note the specific description of the life of this worker, a description that speaks to the queston of a working lifestyle.

Native Americans, as our native tribes are properly named by immigrants, are developing their own ways of preserving a former lifestyle while working into the mainstream, as the article, "Powwows and Peyote Help Indians Adjust to Life in the Big City" by Susan Margolies indicates. Native Americans are located in many of our large cities, and wherever one lives, the subject of the effect of their lifestyle on other youth could be a rich one to explore.

Note that as far as action ministries are concerned, the article by Rubin could stimulate thinking on whether activism is still a feasible style for youth.

Also, the articles by Fitch and Skinner could provide ideas to those who not only want action, but who want it as Christians. The Gustafson article is obviously pertinent to this issue, too.

Distribution

Local groups will want to order enough copies of *Youth Ministry Notebook VIII* to make effective use of the book. In some cases a single copy might suffice, especially if a leader is gaining ideas for planning sessions that can then be brought before a planning group.

In other cases, groups will want to order several copies, in order that several youth planners may have copies as well. This seems the most sensible approach, because planning, whether of a year or of a single session, usually requires that several persons have information about a particular issue.

Remember, too, that panel members and other resource persons whom the group invites from time to time will want to read articles in order to prepare themselves for the session. Enough copies should be on hand to share the articles in this way and to allow for the inevitable loss of a book or two over a period of months.

Planners are reminded that a lengthy advance time is usually required for obtaining films and other extra resource material.

Contributors

Besides the signed articles, the editor has contributed the questions for discussion and suggestions for use at the end of each article, as well as the interview with C. Eric Lincoln. Gary W. Martin, secretary for youth ministry, The United Presbyterian Church in the United States of America, also contributed to the procedures at the end of the articles, and Richard and Kirkie Gibson of Raleigh, North Carolina, provided the information about films, games, and other resources listed at the end of each article.

CHARLES E. COLE, Editor

Marriage and Its Variations

BY PATRICIA DE ZUTTER

Sandy and Garth Matthes see a lot of each other—that's the way they want it. "Garth is my husband, my lover, and my friend," says Sandy. He is also her working partner. The two are founders and directors of a highly successful therapeutic community for drug addicts.

In some ways Garth and Sandy have a traditional, close, one-to-one marriage relationship. In other ways, their relationship reflects some new ideas about marriage. In wedding vows that they composed themselves they promised to "work on our relationship as long as we both want to."

Other couples are trying other variations on the marriage theme. Ellen and her husband have opened their marriage to additional sexual partners. Ann, her husband, and her infant son lived with another couple and their baby for a year, sharing finances, household tasks, and friendship —everything but sex. Charlotte is living in a commune with a lover who is ten years her junior. Three young women have joined Edward and Mary and their daughters to create a reform-minded community in which children have an equal share in decision-making.

Sociologists tell us that such experimentation is here to stay, the result of several related factors that are changing modern life. Of tremendous importance is the fact that the development of effective methods of contraception (chiefly the pill) has given both women and men greater freedom to decide how they will conduct their personal lives. With the baby burden diminished, more women are holding jobs and holding them longer. And a woman with a paycheck in her purse has a greater choice in determining her own lifestyle. Other factors include affluence; availability of more leisure time; the loneliness of a mobile, urban population; disenchantment with established ways, and the influence of the women's liberation movement and other human-growth movements.

Most people still choose a conventional lifestyle —husband, wife, and children living together in their own home or apartment. A high percentage of divorced couples remarry and reestablish conventional lifestyles. Still, sociologists and others suggest that the emerging new styles of marriage and family life are worth looking at. Psychologist

Carl Rogers in his book *Marriage and Its Alternatives* bemoans that, while experimentation is prized in every other area of human endeavor, people engaged in exploring new kinds of intimate partnerships are condemned. He writes:

> Suppose we passed a law which declared that any partnership pattern entered into by mutually consenting adults is now legal, providing it does no clear injury to other persons. This would make for honest, rather than clandestine explorations, and would let these laboratories in partnerships operate openly and honestly.

Echoing these sentiments in a personal way, a young woman said, "I don't want to dislike anyone just because their lifestyle is different from mine."

When Sandy and Garth met at an institute for group and family therapy in California, each had already experienced some deep changes in lifestyle. After conquering his own drug habit, Garth was running a drug rehabilitation center in a small town in California. Sandy, the divorced mother of two children, was a former teacher working in counseling. "We started out knowing a great deal about each other because each of us was at the institute to work on ourselves. That cut through the facade that people erect during courtship. We saw each other for real from the beginning," says Garth.

Sandy comments, "We wanted to keep seeing each other, exploring our relationship step by step, living in the here and now. Not having fantasies about what might happen."

At the end of the summer, Garth returned to Kansas City, Missouri, with Sandy and moved in with her and her children. "When we decided we wanted to marry, we knew we were already married inside our guts—a ceremony wouldn't change that commitment," says Garth.

To some extent, the wedding was a bow to public opinion, Garth admits. Trained in counseling and group therapy, they wanted to work together as a team. "We wanted to be honest with ourselves and our clients, and we knew it would turn some people off if they knew we were living together without being married. And our wedding was a way of saying to our friends, 'This is where we are with each other—this is the way we are going to live.'" Sitting on the floor with the children, their dog, and a few friends, they were married at home by a friend who is a minister. That was three years ago. The following year they started their therapeutic community assisted by state and federal funds for rehabilitation of drug addicts.

Garth, 28, is slim and goodlooking with dark, curly hair and beard and alert, humorous eyes. Sandy has long, brown hair, a friendly smile, and a confident manner. Each wore jeans, shirt and sandals when interviewed in a small parlor at the aging apartment building they converted to house the community they call "Renaissance West."

"What Sandy and I have is rare—not everyone wants what we have," says Garth. "I want a partner I can share everything with—somebody I can feel the ultimate amount of closeness with. That takes a lot of work and energy, and I'm willing to invest a lot of myself in my relationship with Sandy. In our personal relationship and in our work here, we are creating an environment in which it is safe to be straight—to be honest and open with each other and to respect each other."

"I respect Garth—where he is, what he is doing with himself, and what he is doing professionally," responds Sandy. "So many people try to control each other rather than respect where the other is with himself. People try to possess instead of letting themselves unconditionally love and unconditionally receive love."

"We have chosen a one-to-one relationship because that's the way we want it," says Garth. "I am not willing to take energy away from my relationship with Sandy to maintain another intimate relationship. Plenty of times I have fantasies—feelings of attraction to another woman. For me, that's okay. I enjoy my fantasies and my feelings. When it comes time to make a decision to act on my fantasy, I have other things to take into consideration—including what it might take away from Sandy and me."

"I don't believe another woman can take Garth away from me," says Sandy. "He's not a piece of property that someone can take. If I'm having a hassle around jealousy, it may be a thing I haven't worked out for myself rather than another person. I don't believe that people just fall in love—it's gradual. If Garth or I am beginning to fall in love with someone else, that's a cue to me to look at what's going on between Garth and me. I may be

having a hassle with myself and my behavior may be affecting Garth. When things are right between us, I may find myself being attracted to another man, but that's it."

"When we look at what's going on between us, there's always the possibility that it may be necessary to do some redeciding. That's one of the risks," says Garth.

Sandy nods, "I feel that way too."

In discussing their ways of reacting when one or the other is involved with an internal hassle, Garth and Sandy reveal their training as therapists. They are willing to give each other space, time, and support in working out a problem and steadfastly refuse to play rescuer.

"When I have something going on inside, I'm not content with me and not fun to be with," says Sandy. "Usually my internal hassles involve using old ways of surviving—putting in the here and now some manipulative thing I used in the past. I'm trying to control so I don't lose something, instead of accepting and working through a situation that is not mine to control."

"When Sandy is uptight, I feel that," says Garth. "I don't make it my problem. Part of my acceptance of her is letting her have her hassles. My commitment is to be available to her, to give her feedback, to lend her my ears."

"If Garth has a hassle and it's affecting me, I lay it out straight to him," Sandy responds. "I'm not into protecting him from feeling hurt or uptight. If I think he's messed up, I tell him. If I don't want to be with him, I tell him. It's all right to be angry and turned off by each other. It's all right to have something going on inside."

"There is no way to work on a relationship directly," says Garth. "I can work on what I'm doing that gets in the way of being close. I've done a lot of growing by working through the hassles I brought with me into our relationship. The more work I do, the more I see Sandy for what she is, instead of putting my mother's or my grandmother's face on her. This means I leave myself open to getting to know her better."

"We are both growing towards our own autonomy within our relationship," says Sandy. "Part of this is being aware of ways we choose to be dependent on each other. When we do something together, it's because we choose to do it that way—not because we have to have someone to lean on."

Standards for judging the success of a marriage are changing. Not long ago a couple could consider their marriage successful if they stayed together, achieved a measure of financial security, and educated their children. If they enjoyed each other's company in the process, they were exemplary.

Today there is a greater emphasis on personal growth for both marriage partners. Nena and George O'Neill, in their best seller *Open Marriage,* insist that the personal, intellectual, and emotional growth of each partner benefits the other and their marriage. They favor "undependent living" in which each partner has freedom to develop his individual interests and individual friendships in an atmosphere of open communication and mutual trust. They deplore traditional husband and wife "roles" as inhibiting personal development.

The O'Neills view outside sexual relationships as an option in an open marriage. They admit that such action can be risky, but suggest that risks can be minimized by honesty, concern, and consideration for everyone involved. They quote sophisticated, career-oriented couples discussing the satisfactions of "open companionship," but no one in their book says, "We are having mutually agreed upon outside sexual relationships and this is what it is like."

For Ellen, life has become surprisingly painful since she and her husband, Ned, agreed to sex outside of marriage. Ellen has several continuing sexual partners. Ned shares sex with one other woman and the depth of that relationship scares Ellen.

"I am moving through a series of stages, struggling with my own need for support and security," she says.

"When I told Ned I wanted additional sexual relationships, I encouraged him to find another woman to relate to. I thought, 'As long as I am first in Ned's life, I don't care who is second or third.' I don't want to be at that place anymore. I want to relate to people as people—not firsts, seconds, or thirds. I am there in my head, but at a whole different place in my gut. Ned has told me that when he is with me, I am most important. And when he is with her, she is most important. Now I say, 'Ned lives with me and cares about me.'"

Ellen, a vivacious blond of 27, has an interesting job that takes her out of the city several nights a week. She and Ned reserve weekends for each other and their six-year-old son.

"I know a traditional marriage is not for me," she says. "It doesn't meet my needs. I can't be all things to one person, and one person can't be all things to me. I like sexual variety and this is where I want to be. I am aware that this involves the risk of loss. Ned and I may decide not to live together. Our relationship has shifted so much, I feel out on a limb."

Jim, a recent art school graduate, and his wife, Jane, have a number of sexual friendships. Both insist that additional sexual partners don't threaten their marriage. Jane says, "Our relationship with each other is by far the most important relationship. I don't see the possibility that another relationship could ever catch up."

"We were on the verge of divorce when we decided to change our style of marriage," Jim says. "Now we have a good feeling of commitment to each other. We have very open communication and try desperately to stop jealousy feelings when they occur."

To support their primary relationship with each other, Jim and Jane decided to get to know each other better through a series of marathon conversations that lasted all Friday night and most of Saturday. "The more our eyelids drooped, the more honest we became. Because we were willing to reveal our inner selves, we were able to build trust," Jim says.

An obvious question is whether the effort to get to know each other better could have brought excitement and closeness to Jim and Jane's relationship without outside sexual activity.

Couples who favor consensual outside sex suggest that such agreements permit a marriage to continue and grow rather than breaking up as a result of extramarital sex activity. However, the arrangement offers built-in invitations to trouble if both partners are not equally outgoing, attractive, self-confident, and willing.

A community worker comments, "I've talked with ten or fifteen people who say they are practicing consensual outside sex. And what they are saying about how good it is doesn't check out with the pain I am hearing and feeling from them. I haven't seen anybody yet who can handle it. *Open Marriage* has some good ideas in it, but it seems to me that too many people are using it as an excuse to do what they have been wanting to do."

While the O'Neills saw outside sex as an option in an open marriage, others see it as a new standard. A thirty-year-old technical writer, mother of two preschool children, comments, "My husband and I love each other and don't want sex with others. But everybody says you should be liberated. It's a problem."

A further question deals with hurt to others. Jim and Jane revealed a somewhat exploitative attitude as they described how they would react if their outside sexual activity contributed to the break up of another marriage. "I would feel that was the responsibility of the two people involved in that marriage. I can't take responsibility for keeping someone else's marriage intact," Jim said.

Jane agreed, "I'm not willing to pick up a big load of someone else's responsibility. I have withdrawn from that kind of situation."

James W. Ramey, director of the Center for the Study of Innovative Life Styles in New City, New York, suggests that a large part of current experimentation with marriage styles results from efforts of affluent, educated, highly mobile couples to find ways to replace kin, neighbor, and friendship structures no longer available to them on a long-term basis. Ramey's description fits Bill and Sue Smith and Ann and Ted Brown. When Bill and Sue decided to move to Kansas City from California, they knew they wanted to work out a group living arrangement with their long-time friends, Ann and Ted, former California residents.

After planning by mail, the two couples rented a comfortable, modern house in the suburbs. While the husbands worked, the wives shared daily tasks, talked and cared for their infant sons. "Our companionship kept us from the loneliness and boredom so many young mothers feel when they are alone all day with a baby," says Ann.

The two couples found that, in addition to offering companionship, their living arrangement was efficient and economical. The four adults regularly cleaned the entire house in one hour one evening a week. They paid rent on one house rather than two and operated one car. They designed and built a $42,000 dreamhouse, doing much of the finishing work themselves.

Their experiment in group living succeeded, Ann says, "because we cared about each other as individuals." She describes the two-couple relationship as group marriage because they shared finances, shared a commitment to each other, and lived in the same house. She adds that their relationship would not fit most sociologists' definition of group marriage because the two couples did not relate to each other sexually.

Soon after the move to the new house, it became evident that Bill and Sue were encountering serious problems in their seven-year-old marriage. "It's hard to say why two people can't live together—perhaps for Bill and Sue it was different value systems," comments Ann. "I had never before realized how difficult it is to decide to end a marriage. At times it seemed to overwhelm them

—they came close to the decision and then put it off. They struggled with that decision for three months."

When Bill and Sue agreed to separate, the two couples moved quickly to end their experiment in group living. They disposed of the communal car and sold the house for $50,000, sharing close to $8,000 profit. Sue and her son returned to California and Bill moved to another state.

"Our year together was a time of growing for each of us," says Ann. "I think the open communication among the four of us and the support and acceptance that Ted and I were able to give helped Bill and Sue to reach their decision. They feel the decision was good. There is no hostility or bitterness between them. They see each other several times a year and their son spends time with his dad. Neither has remarried."

Bill's and Sue's experience illustrates a prediction by psychologist Herbert A. Otto writing in *The Futurist* magazine:

I expect that the man and woman of the future will face the end of a marriage or love relationship with more equilibrium, and with a greatly diminished sense of trauma, guilt and anxiety or depression. They will recognize that, up to a point, a man and a woman may contribute to each other's growth; but that at a certain juncture, for complex reasons, they may begin to grow apart.

Because they are feeling less pain themselves, the separating couple of the future may have more energy to deal with their children's feelings. At the present time few children are receiving the help they need to deal with such a crisis. A psychotherapist remarks, "I would like to start a therapy group for the children of divorced parents. Often parents are getting a lot of help from counselors and therapy groups. But who is working with the children? Who is saying to them, 'Yes, this has happened. Now, how do you work through your pain and disappointment to where you want to be with yourself?' "

A growing number of couples are avoiding divorce courts by working through their problems with the aid of counseling and therapy groups. Emily and Tom, the parents of four children, decided to seek counseling after sixteen years of marriage. Although they had a stable, caring relationship, they were frequently angry with each other, they didn't communicate well, and their moments of closeness and fun often ended in squabbles. As members of a once-a-week therapy group, they were able to confront fears, catastrophic expectations, and irrational ways of thinking that they had brought to their marriage from troubled childhoods. As they worked through personal and relationship hassles, they learned to recognize their needs and feelings and to communicate them. They developed new skills for solving day-to-day problems and found new creative energy and greater joy in being together.

"I see this type of change as a real alternative lifestyle," comments Richard Nadeau, a transactional analysis therapist. "Each partner has said to the other, 'I care about you and want to be with you; and I care enough to want to be with you differently.' The changes Emily and Tom are making can offer their children some new options in their ways of relating."

For many women the end of the child-raising years means time to return to college or start a new career. Charlotte, 45, chose both and met a handsome young lover. Charlotte traces a progression of self-development through her seventeen-year marriage contracted at age 18 followed by a second four-year marriage. "I have become more myself," she says. In preparation for moving to Mexico with her lover where she will write a thesis for an advanced degree, Charlotte has resigned her administrative job at a college. Moving into and out of the college job, she sees as another example of her progression.

Charlotte doesn't flaunt her unconventional lifestyle. "Some people at the college knew about it. The president knew," she says softly. She admits to a dilemma when introducing her lover to acquaintances. "If I say he is my lover, people are shocked. To describe him as my friend doesn't satisfy me because he is much more than that."

Although her first marriage was troubled for years, Charlotte remained in it for the sake of her three children and because of a need to convince herself she had done all she could to save it. When her second marriage became strained because of differences in interests, values, and daily patterns of behavior, she concentrated on saving the relationship rather than the marriage. As a result, she and her second husband remain friends. Her children (the youngest now 16) live together in California, developing unconventional lifestyles of their own.

Charlotte lived for eight months in a seventeen-member commune that split because of inability to handle conflicts. "Some folks who couldn't talk about their problems retreated to the third floor of our big house," she recalls. "If someone is upset, I want to hear about it. I don't want to go on tiptoes, being sensitive. When the air gets charged, things blow up. Then it's hard to find an effective remedy."

Now in a commune with her lover and three other persons, Charlotte sees honesty and confidence in self and others as being vital to any set of living arrangements.

Edward and Mary are involved in a different type of commune. Theirs is not a commune for companionship or economy, although these factors are important. Their "Christian intentional community" is primarily an experiment in radical social change.

Edward, a college professor who has long been concerned about social issues, describes their family-community as an answer to the question: How do you stay healthy and sane in one of the most immoral lands that God ever watched go down the drain?

"We were angry," says Edward, "angry about this nation's militaristic foreign policy—about the competitive, affluent society that lives off the poor and intimidates people. For us, a subsistence life is the only moral way to avoid contributing to the problem. We have moved from viewing American society negatively to creating a very positive alternative lifestyle."

One of their objections to American society is that minority group members, the poor, the young, the aged, and women, are frequently shut out of the decision-making process in questions that affect them. Likewise, the young, the aged, and women are denied access to the decision-making process in many families. Setting up a way to share power and decision-making was one of the community's crucial early decisions. The group chose a weekly community meeting at which "each member has an equal say and the insights of a child are valued as much as the experiences of an adult."

Nine-year-old Debbie explains what happens when she wants a new pair of jeans. "I talk to the two people who are the clothing committee. They say, 'Do you need them?' and we talk about it. Then they decide. If they say no and I still think I need the jeans, I can bring it up at a community meeting."

Debbie and her twin sister are the two youngest members of the community that includes their other sisters, ages 10, 14, and 17. The three other members are a young woman of 18 and a former nun and a woman minister.

"We would like to have more men in the community," says Edward. "This isn't something you recruit for. Our members are the people who wanted to join us. We are open to additional members."

According to a community decision, the group will take time for "rethinking and restruggling" each time a new member is added. "It will be an opportunity to go back and make sure we are where we want to be," says Edward.

The community began when Edward and Mary, their daughters and the woman minister spent a year in a western state. The children developed their own educational curriculum, drawing on the resources of the valley in which they lived. "Now, going to school seems so restricted," comments Louise, the eldest daughter. "We are told what to study in school, the teachers make all the decisions, and out of school our time is controlled by school assignments." Members of the community hope to start an alternative educational program to assist young people who drop out or are suspended from the city schools operated in their white working-class neighborhood.

Before returning to Kansas City, community members visited communes in other parts of the nation to gather and share ideas. "It was a wonderful year," comments Louise wistfully. She wears jeans and long hair like many girls of 17 but her manner is unusually mature and confident.

A typical day for the community begins with early breakfast prepared by a team of family members. (Household tasks are shared and rotated on a five-day cycle.) With the community gathered at the breakfast table, there is time for communal prayer, newspaper and other current reading, and discussion. Members share their plans and hopes for the day before leaving for school, jobs, or volunteer work. The community gathers again for the evening meal. After that there is time to be together or to attend meetings of interest.

"We are building an arena of support and caring," says Edward. "If someone has a problem, it's everybody's problem. We see community members growing and making incredible movement. We have a banner that says it well, 'Unfolding means pain and joy.'"

Another variation of lifestyles involves homosexual relationships. *Trends* magazine published by the United Presbyterian Church, U.S.A., devotes its July–August 1973 issue to a full discussion of homosexuality. The editors view their subject not as a sin or a sickness but as a variant sexual preference.

For many years Fred, 56, has kept the fact of his homosexual preference hidden from all but a few close friends. Now, active in local and national gay organizations, Fred has begun to talk about his homosexuality with members of the straight community in hopes of building a climate of understanding and acceptance for himself and others.

Fred is currently at a point of crisis in his relationship with his 26-year-old lover, Terry. "We don't communicate well—never have. He wants me home when he is home, but he leaves me out of his social and emotional life. I'm not a dirty old man. Terry initiated our courtship and I was flattered. I think we are now at a point where we can discuss our problem. We may want to make some changes."

Oddly enough, part of the problem between Fred and Terry results from the easing of society's attitude toward homosexuals. "The kids now go to gay bars and don't feel pressured as much as the older group," Fred says. "They have more people to relate to and are not so eager to develop a long, tight relationship. My lover is at this point. He rejects the idea of conforming to what the heterosexual world would like us to be. Those kids know what they are doing—that they are offending the community. I would have felt guilty about these things when I was young."

Most people over 40 who have a homosexual relationship are monogamous, are professional or semiprofessional, and are hiding, Fred says. "They have intelligence and training and are willing to give up a few things, to settle for a close group of gay friends who are also hiding."

Fred would like to see both church and state recognize homosexual marriages. A church ceremony would offer homosexuals the opportunity to publicly affirm their commitment to each other. State recognition would ease tax and inheritance problems for homosexuals living together. And Fred sees a social plus. "My straight friends have never invited my lover and me as a couple. We can't enjoy the couple identity with other people."

While young homosexuals enjoy some benefits not available to Fred's generation, they face substantial problems, too. Society has long portrayed homosexuals as promiscuous, and homosexuals have often thought of themselves in those terms. While modern society has done little to create mechanisms to help heterosexual couples stay together, for the homosexual couple the problem is even more acute. For them, too, consensual outside sex is an issue.

"There is nothing in the homosexual community to support a couple's desire to stay together," complains Jerry, 23, who has just begun what he hopes will be a beautiful, lasting relationship with Bob, 22. "When Bob and I go to a gay bar I think, 'Most of the people here would like to have what I have. And most would be willing to take away what I have if they could.' We have told each other that we should be free to trick on the side if we want to. I can say that in my head, but not in my gut. That's the way we found each other. I don't want it to be the way we lose each other."

While some people are trying innovative styles of marriage or family life, others are taking a new look at the single life. "Being single is becoming an acceptable and desirable way to be," says Joan. In the midst of an exciting second career, Joan feels good about herself and her life as a single woman.

"One of the reasons that I have developed my strengths and inner being has been that I am single and have had to discover myself in my own right and become adequate for me. I have not stood in anyone's shadow or felt my importance hinged upon being somebody's wife or mother. I don't feel less a woman because I have never married."

Joan considers herself open to marriage. "If I marry it will be because I have found a man I want to walk with through life and we can both continue to grow. It won't be a matter of 'Gee! I have to have someone to make me who I am.'"

Joan, a slender brunette, spent twenty-two years as a Catholic nun during which she taught school and served as a school principal. She now directs a state program aimed at educating the public about the need for prison reform.

Living alone in a suburban apartment, Joan has a wide circle of friends, including married and single people. "I need many, many friends," she says. "I have been able to share in depth with many people, and I have met thousands because I have been a professional woman and because as a single woman I have had great freedom to pursue my interests."

Sexuality, marriage, and family life are for most people intimate, personal, and sensitive issues. Many people choose to deal with these issues in a traditional way. Others are trying approaches that appear more innovative. Still others choose a conventional innovative mix. A lifestyle represents one person's answer to the questions "Who am I?" and "How do I want to structure my close relationships?" When the questions are as basic as that, who is to judge whether someone else has given the "right" answer?

Suggestions For Digging Into The Issue

Discussion Questions

1. After reading the article, what hopes do you have for the conventional "nuclear family"—the two parents with one or more children?

2. Which of the several variations described here seem most like possibilities that you could accept?

3. Do any of the relationships described here seem immoral? Why or why not? What makes for morality, beyond the notion of compliance with a set of rules?

4. Many of the situations described here seem to be giving the participants problems. Is this because their relationship is "unnatural," because it is new, or because of some other reason?

5. What effect does communal living have on children? The case of Charlotte mentions a commune with children—does it seem to be more or less healthy than the average family?

6. How do you feel about homosexual marriages, such as those described by Fred?

7. Do you agree with Joan that "being single is becoming an acceptable and desirable way to be?" What are the advantages and disadvantages of being single?

Resource Persons

Follow up on persons who are just a few years older than those in your group. Find out what their marriage relationships and experiences have been (including those who are single). If possible, find an articulate person known to the group to share his or her experiences and observations about marriage today.

A Weekend Retreat

Consider organizing a weekend retreat or a series of

evening sessions on the theme of "Marriage and Its Variations." The purpose would be to educate adults as well as youth about alternatives today. Your church's offices beyond the local church might be able to suggest resource leaders.

Role Play

Simulate some of the situations described in the article and play out a scene where a decision is being made or persons are engaged in conflict. What would happen to the healthy relationship between Garth and Sandy if one of them chose to work at another job? Suppose one of Ellen's consorts tried to influence her to marry him? And so on.

Additional Resources

Books listed (many are in paperback) are generally available from bookstores and/or local public libraries. Rental and/or sale prices of other Additional Resource items are available from distributors; their addresses are listed at the back of the book.

Feature Films

Two for the Road (color, 110 min. Films Inc.). English couple's ten-year marriage straining at the seams.

Darling (b/w, 122 min. Audio/Brandon). Biting satire of life and love among international "jet set."

Lilith (b/w, 155 min. Audio/Brandon). Story of girl who creates a world of her own—one of boundless love, not limited to age, sex or number.

Klute (color, 115 min. Warner Brothers). Character study of call girl and private eye when their lives intersect.

Nights of Cabiria (subtitles, b/w, 110 min. Audio/Brandon). Prostitute becomes a real and touching human being.

Diary of a Mad Housewife (color, 111 min. Universal). Details of surface relationships, illusions, and mis-understandings that plague a marriage of young sophisticates.

Short Films

Our Changing Family Life (b/w, 22 min. McGraw-Hill). Farm family of 1880s compared with today's family.

Caroline (b/w, 28 min. McGraw-Hill). Questions fundamental features of modern urban/suburban life.

Have I Told You Lately That I Love You? (b/w, 16 min. UCC Office for Audio-Visuals; also Univ. of Southern California). Routine life of middle-class family where conversation languishes.

Al! (color, 4 min. Pyramid). Man-woman relationship seen as bitter struggle.

The Most (b/w, 27 min. Pyramid). Candid study of Hugh Hefner and "playboy" philosophy.

The Playboy (b/w, 38 min. BFC-TV Films). Defines "playboy personality" via extemporaneous vignettes.

Filmstrips

What Is Marriage? (2 parts, color, 30 min. Guidance Associates).

The Future of the Family (2 parts, color, 30 min. Guidance Associates).

Tapes

There Are No Monsters (29 min. CSDI #584).

The Family in Crisis (38 min. CSDI #478).

Barbara—An In-depth Study of an American Prostitute (58 min. Pacifica #133).

Sexual Freedom: The Middle of the Road (59 min. Pacifica #A2098).

The Ethics of Sexual Freedom (55 min. Pacifica #A2099).

Divorce American Style (57 min. Center for Cassette Studies).

Simulation

Marriage Enrichment Program (five 2-hr. sessions, Human Development Institute).

Programmed Instruction

Improving Communication in Marriage (8 sessions, Human Development Institute).

Books

Future of the Family ed. C. Barbeau (New York: Macmillan, Bruce Books).

The New Families: Youth, Communes, and the Politics of Drugs by Ross V. Speck et al. (New York: Basic Books).

Committed for Life: Religious Lifestyles

BY LYNNE FITCH

We live in the middle of a tension between three aspects of our life. The first is who we are, physically, psychologically, and emotionally. The second is where we are physically and geographically, family, hometown, economic level. We can, in later life, change parts of that if we so choose, but in the beginning there is not much that we can do about it. The third is what we believe or do not believe, most importantly, it is what we believe strongly enough to stake everything else on.

The way we work with this tension is our lifestyle. When we do not work it out but go along with what comes to us we have a passive lifestyle. When we work out a lifestyle based on our physical comforts and pleasures we are hedonists. When we live according to spiritual, moral, or ethical beliefs we are living a religious lifestyle. Most of us find ourselves living a mixture of these styles.

Style, for most of us, does not need to be defined. We know *style* when we see it. We know the clothing style of the "Roaring 20s," we envy someone who can move with "style" through a difficult situation. Style means that something, or someone, has a particular flair or characteristic, flavor or taste.

A good deal of thought and time and effort is put into developing the style of clothing we adopt and the hair style we choose. But lifestyle, and particularly religious lifestyle, that's something else. Very little time or energy is put into exploring the possibilities of a lifestyle. Often we know how we do not want to live, but rarely do we know how we do want to live. The particular flair or characteristic or flavor or taste of our life is something that we just slip, or fall into.

It is a luxury to be able to explore possible lifestyles for your own life, a luxury granted to those who have not yet made a commitment to a job or another person or children. It is a luxury to have the freedom to choose without making drastic changes in the life we already have. It is a luxury few people realize they have and fewer still use responsibly. It is a luxury that maybe only young people have. When it is exercised well it can prevent unhappiness in a chosen profession or divorce in a family when one or another person wants to change lifestyle.

If a life is said to have a style, there must be something particular, characteristic, peculiar about it: something that is a common thread, something that sets it apart, something that, even if we take only a single part, a single case, points to the whole. That style must be consistent and continuous, long term, if it is to be called a lifestyle rather than a passing fancy.

In a lifestyle that is called "religious," that characteristic, that peculiarity, is a consistent moral or ethical belief. It is a way of living based on how we should live and act and why we should live and act that way. To carry it to the spiritual level the religious lifestyle ultimately rests on a belief in a Supreme Being (God) or a "higher law." That is, something or Someone greater than the individual life and giving scope and dimension and meaning to the life of the individual.

Organized Religion

Perhaps the most familiar religious lifestyle is that of organized religion: denominations, local churches, religious orders. If there is style, it is marked by definite steps and requirements. Generally speaking there is a lack of spontaneity. One joins a church, participates in committees, listens to sermons. Perhaps one is even called on to practice what is preached.

The local Christian church is a community, a fellowship, an extended family, a family based on faith and belief rather than kinship. It is a community based on the belief that God was revealed to us in human form through Christ Jesus, a community based on the belief that through the life and death and resurrection of Christ Jesus all persons may participate in a new and renewed life. Faith in the renewal of life and the love of God for humanity draws us into a community of love and concern for each other. The foundation of the Christian community is the faith that Christ has come to draw humanity into a healing and renewing relationship with God. The guidelines for building the community and interpreting the faith are the teachings of Christ Jesus and the Bible.

Honestly, the Christian community is also based on the need to keep the organization alive and going: alive and going so that the teachings, the Word, may be shared, alive so that people will have ready channels for their religious life. It is not wrong to say that for many people the excitement, spontaneity, and even spirituality of religion has been dulled by experience with the organization of the local church, that it is not a place where anyone expects to get "turned on." But things are changing.

Things are changing in two specific areas. The first area of change is the rising sense of responsibility people have for themselves and for their own lives. Perhaps the first step in consciously choosing a lifestyle is to claim responsibility for yourself. The dynamic that develops produces a lifestyle based on a common teaching (the Bible), but also claims a person is young or old, male or female, gay or straight, third world or white.

Local churches and large denominational meetings are finding in their midst organizing and powerful caucuses—youth, women, even homosexuals. Each group is asserting that what is sacred about the church and the religious life is not organization, tradition, and polity but the teaching and the faith. They are probing the written word, the Scriptures, for direction for life. They are laying claim to two things: first, the belief that Christ came to give abundant life to all people; and second, the power that resides in the structure of the church.

People are beginning to feel that organization and power are not necessarily bad. They are stating that a religious lifestyle may well be one that attempts to use the existing religious structures for "good" ends. They are claiming responsibility for who and what they are and using that to work on where they are in the world. Importantly too, people are doing this without apology to other social issues or world problems.

It is a sign of psychological and spiritual health to be able to claim who you are and not "put yourself down." It is a sign of health for the church to have its members reaching out to each other for support and strength. It is a sign of health for the church to have its members searching the Scriptures and their own spirituality for meaning and direction for their own lives. It is a sign of health for organization to be reshaped and restructured in line with the reasons for the founding of the structure.

Charismatic Communities

The second area of change within the organized church occurs as a result of, or response to, the growing number of spiritually oriented Christians. It would be difficult to discuss the religious lifestyle without giving some thought to the increasing numbers of charismatic communities. Most Protestant denominations, the Catholic church, and Judaism, too, have felt the force of charismatic Christianity. There are increasing numbers of people who find meaning for life in the evangelical Christian message and lifestyle. There is even a group called Jews for Jesus.

What are the characteristics of this lifestyle? The most obvious is openness to the movement of the "Spirit": spirituality and spontaneity, belief that by not being concerned with the things of the world one can gain eternal life in the spirit, belief that one must totally open life, body, and spirit to being filled by the Holy Spirit. The Holy Spirit will then give direction for life.

A second characteristic of this lifestyle is that of evangelism: sharing the message, going out to all people to tell and share, attempting to convert others, street corner by street corner, door by door.

Another characteristic is that of developing well-disciplined communities: communities that may or may not be existing congregations. For some young charismatics it is a residential community, a Christian commune. Often the community has a coffeeshop or a bookstore that serves as a place to meet others and a means of support for the community. Occasionally the community is made up of former drug addicts or alcoholics who have been reformed and are now concerned with reforming others.

Positively, the charismatic lifestyle reminds us of the need for a strong spiritual dimension to one's existence. There is a need to take time to stop and examine belief and faith, to draw into oneself for rest from the daily routine. Spirituality of any type requires time and discipline. The Trappist monks spend a lifetime learning and practicing the discipline of being prayerful and open to the spirit. Certainly the monks' lifestyle takes a different form, but the importance of the spiritual is there. Mainline Christianity is often impatient and embarrassed with silent prayer or the spontaneity of being open to the Spirit.

Also positively, there is a strong community of support in the charismatic movement. For people who are questioning or searching there is a place. There is a strong emphasis on the need that we have for each other in the religious life.

Negatively, charismatics may be introspective to the point of totally ignoring gross social and political problems. Concern for the physical level of life is abandoned. Unless one is approached on the spiritual level there is little communication. It is only in the areas of drug and alcohol reform that charismatic communities are seen to reach out to social problems.

Also negatively, the support community can be a smother community. It is a well-disciplined life in which one is expected to discipline oneself to the leadership. To question is to express a falling back in the faith. For unstable people, many of whom are attracted to the warmth of these communities, this can be a crushing experience: an experience that causes pain, guilt, and eventually departure from the group.

The Catholic Worker Movement

The charismatics do not have a corner on the spiritual lifestyle. Many people whom the world seems to consider political or social radicals are actually immensely spiritual people. They are people with a strong prayer and meditative life, a prayer life that has led them, rather than speaking in tongues as with some charismatics, to dramatic political or social action.

Some forty years ago a woman named Dorothy Day met a French immigrant named Peter Maurin and the Catholic Worker movement was born. Both were devout Catholics, Dorothy Day a recent convert. Both had been through a strongly personal spiritual journey that had brought them to a desire for a lifestyle based on anarchism, socialism, and pacifism and a belief in the holiness of each human being and the ultimate need for one-to-one contact.

They developed and live in (though Peter Maurin is now dead) communities based on that belief. The Catholic Worker is not a newspaper. It is a score of houses of hospitality located in the ghettos and slums of large cities: houses where destitute people can find food and a bed and help with a job; houses where clergy and laity can go for spiritual retreats or instruction in the spiritual life and practice; houses where people feel the need to look after the needs of each other and practice works of mercy; houses where the pacifist and the conscientious objector can find people with whom to talk, people who can and will provide support.

The Catholic Worker movement has also founded farming communities, such as Tivoli farm in upstate New York, communities where people are able to return to the land, work according to their individual ability, and receive according to need.

Personalistic? Socialistic? Naive in total acceptance of those who come for help? Perhaps. There is no question that Dorothy Day is still at the helm of the movement and that she is a devout Catholic. Her lifestyle is one of prayer and meditation and complete acceptance of those who came to her or to the farm in need.

The Catholic Worker movement and Catholic Worker houses have been the religious birthplace for many people. Ex-Workers are found throughout the Catholic Church, clergy and lay, and around the world. Catholic Workers were and are in the ghettos of the southern United States, on the Bowery in New York City, and in the slums of South America. Catholic Workers are also members of groups who were and are active in pacifist and antiwar movements. Unlike some traditional Christian church people they are willing to stake all that they have on what they believe. Mike Cullen for example.

Mike Cullen came from Ireland to the United States to study for the priesthood when he was 18, but decided to marry instead. He left the seminary and, with his wife, became deeply involved in working with the poor and hungry people of Milwaukee. Following Dorothy Day's example and inspiration, the Cullens opened Casa Maria, a Catholic Worker hospitality house created to house, clothe, and feed the poor. Also, following the Catholic Worker emphasis on pacifism and the sanctity of life, the Cullens engaged in the opposition to United States involvement in the war in Southeast Asia. As a result of his antiwar activity Mike Cullen was deported to his native Ireland. It was reported in the newspaper that as he was leaving the United States he was asked if he would become involved in the troubles in Ireland. Cullen's reply, quoted by Ethel Gintoft in *National Catholic Reporter,* reflects the lifestyle he and his family have adopted: "The world is our home. Ireland is no different than Milwaukee with its pains and joys—maybe Ireland has more pain right now. We will try to live our lives there as we have until now—that is, nonviolently. I feel I will be politically active by living my life nonviolently."

Daniel Berrigan

Also Catholic, also strongly contemplative, pacifist, and no stranger to Dorothy Day, is Daniel Berrigan. What Dorothy Day has chosen to do in a quiet way with an emphasis on the personal needs of individuals Berrigan has chosen to do in a public way with concern for national morality. He is as evangelical as the charismatics.

Berrigan is not alone in his lifestyle, but he is a public figure and so we will use his name and experience. He lives a life based on the sanctity of life: the holiness of life and the need to responsibly claim one's life from the social and political forces that would use it. To know the directions in which to move one must be able to pray and follow the teachings and example of Jesus the Christ. Berrigan blends the traditional teachings and practices of the church with the evangelism, responsibility, and spontaneity of the life open to the movement of the Spirit.

So Berrigan and other political activists have chosen to live a lifestyle that is most frequently on a collision course with "the system." One of the results is that most frequently daily life is lived in community rather than family units. This lifestyle requires the ability to put life, *all*, on the line and not hold back. When family, possessions, goods, children are involved, it is difficult to risk all.

Berrigan has written many books and volumes of poetry. He could be a rich man. Instead, he has chosen to use the profits of his writing to support people whom he has met in prison. When they are released he supports many of them until they are able to support themselves.

The United Farm Workers

There is one other movement in this country which I would like to use to illustrate a religious lifestyle. It is used because it is radical, different. Many would not consider it "religious." Many would think it strange to include a labor union, but this is a very different union. The United Farm Workers, and Cesar Chavez, have a strong religious base. Their base is in traditional church doctrines and in the belief in the worth of human life and the right of each person to live. It is a base in nonviolence and in the dignity of all people before God.

The United Farm Workers combines the evangelism of the charismatics, the personalism and pacifism of the Catholic Worker, the desire to constructively use the power of mainline churches and of the Berrigans' opposition to the dehumanizing systems. Chavez's lifestyle is that of the farmworkers. He was and is a farmworker. Those who work with him live on subsistance wages, no more than those who work in the fields. The hours are long and hard and the expectation is *todo para la causa*, everything for the cause. The cause is the empowerment of human life under God.

Migrant and seasonal farm laborers have long been ill treated and very poorly paid. Through conscious and unconscious actions the growers have discouraged any moves to organize the migrant and seasonal workers. When living and working conditions became so intolerable that the workers began to make demands upon the growers, the workers found that they no longer had jobs. The growers were able to turn to the next group of "accessible poor" and find many people who were willing to work for whatever the growers would give them. The growers found that they always had access to people so poor that they were grateful for any chance to work.

With the organization of the United Farm Workers in 1966 the poor of this nation were given an instrument, a tool, for moving out of the poverty level. It is a tool of their own design and making, and this is why it does not resemble any of the large and well-organized labor unions. It is a force for social reform within which people are able to begin to accept and exercise responsibility for themselves and for other poor people.

But the United Farm Workers is not an accomplished fact. It is a tool still in the process of being established. Growers are still opposed to organized farm labor. There are still very poor people in this country to whom the growers have access. There are still many people for whom a choice of lifestyle is the ultimate in luxury.

The illustrations I have chosen are almost all radical. Perhaps any religious life is radical. Certainly it is radical to cut oneself off from the world and enter a convent or monastery. Certainly it is radical to oppose the existing order. Certainly it is radical to be charismatic and go from door to door urging others to consider their religious life. Certainly it is radical to be consistent in living according to what we believe and not what is easiest. Perhaps it is even radical to consider religion radical.

Conclusion

Basically I draw four points of commonality in the lifestyles that have been mentioned.

The first is the need for a spiritual dimension, be it in private prayer, common worship, or meditation. This requires discipline and practice.

The second, and perhaps one of the most important, is the need for community: community to support and direct the religious lifestyle; a drawing together of loves with a common base for shared life and work.

The third is an "other directedness": A claiming of oneself and a direction toward those around with a desire to act responsibly in terms of social order, needs, or evangelism.

Finally, there is a long-term commitment. In an interview Cesar Chavez once said that he can afford to take time for a spiritual retreat because he is "in this thing for life." There is no sudden victory or change that invalidates the lifestyle for him. Lifestyle is a way of relating to the world, and the working out of that relationship is not a six-day war. It is a long term commitment to a life based on a belief that is not imposed but accepted. It is a lifestyle that cannot be denied and from which we cannot be ejected because it is part of us and we are part of it.

Suggestions For Digging Into The Issue

Discussion Questions

1. How do you feel about the way Christian faith has affected your own style of life? Has it affected it at all, and if it has not, is that bad?

2. To what extent is a religious lifestyle visible and how much of it is interior and spiritual?

3. In what sense are all serious religious movements "radical" and sponsor radical ways of living? How do you respond to the argument that being radical is a matter of serious intent and not of dress or exterior features?

4. What is it in religion that causes some, like the charismatic communities, to emphasize the personal and passive, and others, like Cesar Chavez, to emphasize the social and the active?

5. How universal are some of the examples and models described in this article? For example, is a Daniel Berrigan unique, or is it possible for others to imitate his brand of activism?

6. In what sense is it possible for a person to admire the cause of an activist or moral hero, but deplore the methods used? In what sense are Christians "copping out" if they merely criticize an activist without taking some action to remove an injustice?

Role Play

Ask several persons who have read this article to assume the roles of the various religious lifestyles described. Pose a question and ask each to respond to it to understand how the lifestyle affects attitudes toward basic issues. Some questions that might be explored are: What is the place of religion in American life? Can organized religion (the churches) ever hold forth a radical lifestyle? Are all religiously oriented lifestyles rigid, or can some of them be flexible enough to listen to the world as well as to act on it?

Cause and Effect

The following procedure may help a group to consider the role of religious lifestyle in confronting social issues.

In scientific and technological society and situations we tend to think that each effect we see has a cause or set of causes. This may be true in the laboratory, but in social situations people may not agree about what causes produce a given effect. For instance, mention poverty and one person may say: "If the poor would only quit being so lazy and pull themselves up by their bootstraps, they would not be so poor." Another may say: "Jesus himself said the poor would always be with us." Still another: "A poor person may have quit school to go to work to support his family, a machine may have taken his job, and he or she may have applied for many other jobs without being hired."

Prepare several sheets of newsprint with one effect written at the top. For example: TREE, POVERTY, CRIME, GHETTO, CHURCH, WEALTH, HUNGER, WELFARE. You may think of others. Then ask various members of the group to state the cause for each of these effects from the standpoint of a Native American, a black Muslim, a poor person, a member of the white middle class, an atheist, a Communist, a Christian, and so on. Write the responses in catchwords. Discuss with the group how people's position in society determines their understanding of effects around them. How would someone like Jesus or Amos deal with these effects?

Space Carving

Ask each person in the group to think of the symbol or belief in his or her own religious life that means the most to him or her. Then ask each person to try to communicate the meaning of the symbol or belief by means of "space carving." The rules are that hands, faces, and any part of the body may be used, but no objects and no words. Afterward, talk about the variety of beliefs in the group. If the exercise has been difficult, discuss why this is so and how religion is more a matter of living than of merely talking.

Perhaps the session could lead to other sessions that would examine the differences and the values of religious communities and lifestyles.

Additional Resources

Books listed (many are in paperback) are generally available from bookstores and/or local public libraries. Rental and/or sale prices of other additional Resource items are available from distributors; their addresses are listed at the back of the book.

Feature Film

Marjoe (color, 88 min. Cinema 5). Life of con man on the evangelical circuit.

Short Films

Awareness (color, 22 min. Mass Media). On Buddhism.

Road Signs on a Merry-Go-Round (color, 57 min. UCC Office for Audio-Visuals; also Mass Media). Dialogue on faith in God and in man based on writings of contemporary theologians.

The Holy Ghost People (b/w, 53 min. McGraw-Hill). Explores fundamentalist Pentecostal congregation.

The Mood of Zen (color, 13 min. UCC Office for Audio-Visuals; also Indiana Univ.). Zen Buddhism as method of self-discipline.

The Ultimate Trip (color, 32 min. UCC Office for Audio-Visuals; also NBC). Story of the "Jesus People."

Viva La Causa (color, 22 min. UCC Office for Audio-Visuals). Shows the United Farm Workers with Cesar Chavez and Joan Baez.

Tapes

The Occult and the Supernatural: Experts Probe Youth's Spiritualism and Its Search for a New Faith (42 min. Center for Cassette Studies).

Jesus Is Coming (29 min. Pacifica #BC0800).

Is Atheism the Religion of the Future? (43 min. Pacifica #XX0027).

Zen and Creativity (43 min. Pacifica #XX0027).

Simulation

Discovering Spiritual Values in Community (ten 2-hr. sessions, Human Development Institute). Explores spiritual dimensions of human existence in group life.

Drama

It's Happening Now, Baby (Contemporary Drama). Young couple gets involved with LSD religious cult.

Books

New Gods in America by Peter Rowley (New York: Bobbs-Merrill).

New Religions of American Youth Today (New York: David McKay).

Dick Gregory's Political Primer by Dick Gregory; ed. James R. McGraw (New York: Harper & Row).

Nigger: An Autobiography by Dick Gregory; ed. Robert Lipsyte (New York: Dutton).

The Shadow That Scares Me by Dick Gregory; ed. James R. McGraw (Garden City, N.Y.: Doubleday).

Periodicals

A. Rubin, ed., "Rapping with the Jesus People," in *Senior Scholastic*, December 13, 1971.

J. C. Haughly, "Jesus People of Ann Arbor: Word of God Community," in *America*, February 12, 1972.

Where Have All the Radicals Gone?

BY TRUDY RUBIN

"A really good portion of my friends are dead or underground, the people I identified with and thought were the best people I knew.

". . . We did what was necessary in the 60s. That played out its hand, and now it's time to approach a different situation with experimentation."

—Bo Burlingham, former Weatherman

Yesterday's extremists haven't become today's establisment. But they *have* changed. They are "a little older, a little smarter," to quote one of them, aware now that "you make progress step by step." In an anguished decade, events have forced a shift from the tactics of violence and despair to those of tolerance and hope. But the goals remain: radical changes in society.

In 1969 Bo Burlingham was "running with the Weathermen" through the streets of Chicago, as the radical extremist group smashed windows during its self-styled "days of rage." Today the genial, sandy-haired young man is managing editor of *Ramparts* magazine, a well-known periodical of the Left whose base he is trying to expand to reach the "McGovern constituency."

In 1968, Tom Hayden, one of the best-known radicals of the 1960s and founder of Students for a Democratic Society, was fighting in the streets outside the Democratic National Convention and asserting that the country was on the verge of revolution. In 1972 he advised supporters to work for Sen. Edmund S. Muskie (D) of Maine if necessary to help end the war. Today he heads a new group which says it aims at putting grassroots pressure on Congress to keep the peace and educating local citizens' groups on the meaning of the war.

Local People Organized

In 1970, black-bearded Michael Ansara, the best-known SDS leader in the New England area, helped lead a splinter-SDS march through Harvard Square which left every window in the area broken. Later that year he was beaten by working-class youths in blue-collar Lowell for carrying a Vietcong flag in an antiwar march. Since 1970, Mr. Ansara, his hair neatly trimmed, has lived quietly and organized local people successfully in the blue-collar Dorchester section of Boston.

These young men have not changed their views about the American system. Nor have a score of other former SDS leaders, once members of the best-known radical group of the 1960s. Most of those interviewed have stayed alive in some way, but their tactics and attitudes have been radically changed by events of the past few years.

Some Opt for Communes

Among those still active there is a definite trend toward community organizing around local issues. Others have returned to graduate school or are teaching. Some have become radical professionals. A few have abandoned active politics, moving to rural communes. One ex-Weatherwoman is reported to have signed a book contract recently to write about her experiences—with a $12,000 advance.

SDS as a national organization is moribund, its demise paralleling the disappearance of campus revolts. Its violence-bent Weatherman faction has disintegrated. In 1970 three young people were killed in the explosion of a New York townhouse "bomb factory." Most of the remaining top leadership has disappeared underground, eluding the FBI for three years and heard from only occasionally in 1971 via bombings for which they claimed responsibility. Only small chapters of a doctrinaire Maoist SDS faction remain on some campuses.

Among the former SDSers who continue to work, there is a definite shift in attitude. There is clearly a new tolerance toward opposing opinions and a more sanguine assessment of their own powers. Gone is the apocalypticism of the '60s— the dream of revolution around the corner.

"When I was a Weatherman there was a heady period when it looked in 1968 like the youth of the world was rising up," recalls Bo Burlingham. "We were incapable of thinking in terms of twenty years." Now he feels that radical social change in his lifetime is "really problematic . . . though possible."

Tactics Have Changed

Mr. Burlingham, a 1968 graduate of Princeton University, spent the year of the 1968 Paris uprising in France on a Fulbright scholarship and joined the Weathermen after a trip to Cuba in the summer of 1969. He is under indictment with fourteen others (most of them underground) on charges of conspiring to bomb police facilities in four cities in 1970—although he left Weatherman before its underground-bombing stage began.

Although his outrage has not diminished at the injustices he feels America commits, his tactics have changed. "The movement got itself into a situation where it was unable to talk with anyone else," he says.

Mr. Burlingham does not feel the radicals of the '60s failed. He argues that more ordinary people are aware of injustice now. "The important thing is to nurture that, to make sure there is a bridge between the '60s and the next period of upheaval." He hopes to find in *Ramparts* a new means of communicating to a broader audience.

Of Bo's friends from the '60s who are aboveground, most, he says, "have retained some link with the past." Of his three Weatherman co-defendants who are aboveground, one is putting out a prisoners' newsletter in New York City, one woman is contemplating medical school, and the third—also a woman—is living with a group of women on a farm in Arkansas, after playing in a women's rock band. Other friends, he says, "have gone back to school and become radical intellectuals."

"Establishment" Avoided

Bo earns $700 a month at his job, hardly luxury, but a far step above the self-imposed poverty of SDS. He lives in an apartment with his wife, Lisa, a former SDS organizer who is now active in women's health work, and their son, Jacob, 15 months. He is adamant that he will not slip quietly into the white middle-class establishment.

"I feel like I don't want to be part of the mainstream. There was a whole generation who learned too much about America. We have different ways of coping. Some drop out and live on farms, some write or edit magazines, some go on teaching. But what we learned is indelibly imprinted."

High School Campaigning

Michael Ansara is an SDS leader who made the journey from Harvard and the student mecca of Cambridge to a working-class Dorchester section of Boston. Mr. Ansara has been active politically since he was in high school eleven years ago. At that time he campaigned for a nuclear-disarmament candidate. He was well known as an active organizer in national and New England SDS in the late '60s. Although he criticized Weatherman and never joined, he was a mover behind the November Action Council, which staged the destructive march on Harvard Square in April 1970.

For the past three years, Mr. Ansara and his wife, Amy, have lived in white, working-class Dorchester. They have helped build a local movement called The People First; led an apparently effective crusade against a highly unpopular district judge, and against the intrusion of a branch of the state university; and generated a visible amount of opposition to the Vietnam war. Similar organizing is being done by former SDS colleagues of the Ansaras in several depressed blue-collar cities near Boston.

Movement Called "Inbred"

Mr. Ansara and his wife—who is also an organizer but currently supports them by nursing—have committed their lives for the foreseeable future to organizing. But Mr. Ansara feels he has learned a lot from the '60s and from Dorchester. "One of the reasons I moved to Dorchester," he says, "was because I was sick of the movement. It was so inbred with no desire to reach out to other people. I've learned that if you respect people with different opinions and put information in a form accessible to them, they are tremendously open. . . ."

Unlike SDS days, Mr. Ansara sees a need now for "more stress, not on action but on digging in, having skills people want, not just technical but political." He says radicals must overcome their suspicion of good organization and must help local groups form mass organizations to democratize the police, courts, city councils, and other local institutions.

Close Friends Scattered

His time framework, too, has changed from the days when SDS demanded "immediate transformation from where we were to where we wanted to be."

"Now I'm a little older, a little smarter," he says. "I realize you make progress step by step. There will be phases, but each time you trap a little sand, and when the next upsurge comes in a period of crisis, you are that much higher on the shore. . . ."

Mr. Ansara says his close friends from Harvard and SDS of 1968–69 have scattered four ways: "One group has left the city and is doing stuff around the country, working health clinics, community organizing, working in plants, lots of people teaching in working-class colleges, some radical doctors and lawyers. A second group has stayed active around here. A third still thinks it is part of the Left, but is more into identity crises than political work except for attending demonstrations. And a tiny group has gone into doctrinaire Marxist sects."

Local Activity Favored

Of those top SDS officials still active, the trend is toward social activity.

The last three SDS presidents—Mark Rudd, Michael Klonsky, and Bernardine Dohrn—have all disappeared underground, with Miss Dohrn

reputed to be in Algeria. Of early SDS officials, Al Haber, a cofounder, is a carpenter, living in a commune in Berkeley. Paul Potter, an early president, has become an ascetic, according to friends, and has written "an introspective book."

Paul Booth, national secretary in 1965–66, heads a highly successful grass-roots tax-revolt organization in Chicago called Citizens' Action Program (CAP). Mr. Booth, who believed back in his SDS days that the group should organize grass roots rather than students, has led successful CAP campaigns against a crosstown expressway and under-assessed steel mills. Now his group is taking on property taxes statewide.

Perhaps most interesting is the change in Tom Hayden. Although he openly distrusts electoral politics, he has come to accept it as a necessary area of political pressure. And he has also strongly rejected the hatred toward the United States which marked so many of his speeches a few years ago. "We have overcome a lot of hatred that was falsely aimed at the country and not at the government," he said in an interview. "How can you organize a majority of people in a country to hate their country?"

Mood of Entrenchment

The overwhelming mood expressed by these young men was a sense of waiting. Writing in a recent issue of *Ramparts,* long-time chronicler of the left, Andy Kopkind, expressed it like this:

"The mood I feel most often from people who think of themselves "in the movements" is entrenchment—not despair or surrender (although there's enough of that) but digging in. Digging into residential communities, into working places, into tolerable and tolerant jobs, into research, into hip media, into communal life, into self-understanding.

It feels to me like a waiting time. . . . Having finished with the politics of fantasy and having rejected the politics of despair, the only prospect now is hope."

Trudy Rubin is a staff writer for the *Christian Science Monitor.* Her article appeared originally in that publication, February 23, 1973, as the first of its series on radical activists. It is reprinted here by permission.

Suggestions For Digging Into The Issue

Discussion Questions

1. What do the student radicals of the 1960s have in common with Christians? For instance, how would Christians view "radical" change—change that strikes at the roots of injustice or evil?

2. Because of the radicals of the 1960s, is the present generation of high school and college students markedly different? For instance, are today's students more or less conservative? What factors other than the radicals have affected the stance of today's students?

3. Are there radicals (of any age or kind) in your community? What are their methods and goals? Would it be appropriate for youth in a church to communicate with them? To join with them in action? How do these groups compare with foreign activists like Al Fatah, the I.R.A., and the Jewish Defense League?

4. Why are middle-class Christians so reluctant to engage in direct action to resolve injustice?

5. What are the most significant problems facing society today? Brainstorm the question; then go back and ask: What methods would be most effective in solving these problems? For instance, what is the best way to overcome poverty: through political organization? individual actions? economic activity? study? or religious means (prayer, for example)?

6. What are the effects of radical activist groups, such as the Weathermen, the SDS, and the Black Panthers, on society? Ask one person or a small group of persons to look up articles and news stories on these and/or other radical activist groups (Newsweek, Time, Ramparts, Life, among other magazines, might be good sources) and report on them to the total group. Then have the total group discuss the question of the radicals' effects on society.

Organize for Action

If the group becomes "turned on" by the prospect of action, identify an issue that is important enough to work on, but within the dimensions of the group's resources. Get organized and go to work and see what can be done. If there is a professional community organizer in your community, it would undoubtedly be helpful to have his or her help on what to do and not do to be effective. But whether you are successful or not in your action, an evaluation will enable individuals to learn from the experience.

Enlist as Volunteers

Another alternative, a more realistic one for most groups, is to locate organizations working on issues or goals that members of your group feel are important. Then throw your support to them as a way of solving the problem. For instance, if racism is the issue, the National Association for the Advancement of Colored People or the Urban League can help. Almost all national organizations have local chapters or at least chapters of local participants.

Additional Resources

Books listed (many are in paperback) are generally available from bookstores and/or local public libraries. Rental and/or sale prices of other Additional Resource items are available from distributors; their addresses are listed at the back of the book.

Feature Film

If (color, 111 min. Films Inc.). Part humorous, part realistic, part revolutionary tale about English private school life.

Short Films

Hypothese Beta (color, 7 min. McGraw-Hill). Can one be a nonconformist without destroying society?

Confrontation (color, 3 reels: 32 min., 25 min., 29 min., respectively, NBC). Exploding forces on the campus.

Anatomy of Violence (b/w, 30 min. Indiana Univ.). Presents speeches on relationship of violence to social reform.

Tapes

The Gulf in 1980 (26 min. CSDI #424).

A Moral Equivalent for Riots (29 min. CSDI #295).

The Radical Movement (57 min. Pacifica #BC0530).

Roots of American Radicalism (27 min. Center for Cassette Studies).

People's Park—A Documentary (59 min. Pacifica #AP1222.01).

History and Aims of the S.D.S. (45 min. Pacifica #AL1449).

Books

Will the Revolution Succeed? by E. Schwartz (New York: Abelard-Schuman).

Contemporary Radical Ideologies by A. J. Gregor (New York: Random House).

Thought of the Young Radicals (New York: Pitman).

The American Experience: A Radical Reader ed. Harold Jaffe and John Tytell (New York: Harper & Row).

The New Revolutionaries ed. Tariq Ali (Boston: Little, Brown).

Soledad Brother: The Prison Letters of George Jackson by George Jackson (New York: Coward, McCann & Geoghegan).

Blood in My Eye by George Jackson (New York: Random House).

The Movement Toward a New America ed. Mitchell Goodman (New York: Knopf).

Custer Died for Your Sins by Vine Deloria, Jr. (New York: Avon).

We Talk, You Listen by Vine Deloria, Jr. (New York: Dell).

Case Study of a Commune

BY CHARLIE SKINNER

When one hears the word "commune," words that frequently come to mind are "sex," "drugs," and "young people." Anyone who has ever lived in a commune and has had dialogue with the broader society has had to answer questions about these subjects. Though communes do have to seriously consider these questions, other factors are, I believe, much more basic and important.

What Is a Commune?

To me a commune is a group of individuals who have decided to live together cooperatively holding a common intentionality to share personal aspects of their individual and group lives while sharing in the economics of food and housing. The size, duration, degree, and intensity of economic and personal sharing may vary considerably from group to group.

My participation in communal living grew out of a house church group that began meeting to focus on the topic of communes at Chicago Theological Seminary in the autumn of 1970. What these meetings accomplished was to allow the group to get to know each other very well and to develop a style of interaction and effective and meaningful communication. It was not until the very end of the school year in 1971 that serious consideration was given to living together. Thus, the better part of a year was spent developing interpersonal relationships and creating a strong base for community prior to the formal beginning of Covey House in September 1971. Having been a member of the community from its beginning at C.T.S., I lived at Covey House for one year until I returned to seminary to finish my degree.

Covey House began as a commune, or community, of eleven individuals, five women and six men, living in one household (in Nashville, Tennessee). The eleven of us lived together in a twenty-room house, which included nine bedrooms and three bathrooms, that we rented. We shared the cost of rent, electricity, and other utility bills, which amounted to $50 per person per month. We bought food and cleaning supplies together, amounting to an additional $5 per person per week. On trips taken together the cost of gas was shared by all except the driver who had to pay basic upkeep.

All routine household tasks were shared. Two people cooked each meal and two people washed dishes according to an eleven-day list. Two people bought grocery supplies each week. For half of the first year we used a similar type of list for housecleaning, but then divided the house up so that individuals were responsible for the same section of the house each week, such as kitchen or living room. To sign up to carry out these tasks meant that that person was responsible for seeing that his or her chore got done. This often meant an exchange of job times. For example, often by the end of eleven days almost every name on the cooking washing list had been crossed out and changed to a different time. Sometimes another person would take over the task completely. So there was much flexibility in accomplishing the shared work.

The only other scheduled group responsibilities were for each person to try to be present at the evening meal (though often some were not) and to be present at the weekly meeting for business and interpersonal relations. This meeting was the heart of community life; it was the vehicle for growth and change, problem solving, and maintaining meaningful and effective communication. Decisions here were usually made by consensus. If, however, consensus could not be reached, a "sensitive democracy" functioned in which the majority opinion usually ruled, but special attention was given to the minority position. Although I cannot think of a single time that we did not reach a consensus while I was there, one situation which reflects the idea of a sensitive democracy occurred at the very beginning when we were discussing responsibilities. Chris was not interested in shopping, but had been handling some of the finances for the group before it formally began, so it was agreed that she would handle the finances and in turn would not have to do any grocery shopping.

Many hours and chores were shared at Covey House, yet there were times when individual initiative and privacy were foremost concerns. We did not share EVERYTHING! Though virtually all possessions were individually owned, many were shared with the group, including stereos, TV, and cars. Anything a person did not wish to share, such as a favorite chair or a lamp, was kept in private rooms. Community jobs (outside of those mentioned earlier), such as the caring for the lawn, and the garden, repairing the washer and dryer, painting, and remodeling, were done by the person with those skills or the one most interested in getting the work done. If the one or ones with a skill tired of doing the work all the time, they would show another person how to do it or ask for help. Sometimes people bought things for the house with their own money, such as a set of dishes or a rocking chair, for everyone's enjoyment.

At Covey House many similarities in backgrounds and beliefs were shared by the individuals, but there was a strong respect for individual differences. It was this respect for each other's differences, I believe, in combination with a ready willingness to take responsibility for sharing and standing up for one's own thoughts, ideas, and feelings that allowed Covey House to function well. There were occasional conflicts in the house, but these did not become buried or pushed aside. We tried to deal with them openly and honestly, usually in our weekly meetings. For example, the change from week-by-week housecleaning to regular cleaning of selected rooms by individuals was the resolution of a conflict between Dick and me about how he was cleaning the house.

The success of interaction was perhaps due in part to the skill and understanding of methods of counseling, gestalt therapy, encounter, and transactional analysis that most people in the group had, believed in, and practiced. It is important to note, however, that the interaction was characterized not as a counseling or therapy group but as friends freely, willingly, and openly sharing ideas and feelings with each other.

Interpersonal relationships had aspects of both marriage and family living. To the surprise, and satisfaction, of several of us, the only sexual sharing that went on with the group was characterized by the typical dating pattern that one finds in society today. There was not any competition in this dating inside or outside the house, but rather a real respect for the relationships that did exist, whatever state they were in. In fact, on a day-by-day basis, the individuals related primarily as brothers and sisters on good terms.

Life in any community has a lot to do with the people in it and the work they do. Steve was a student from Chicago Theological Seminary who ran Nashville's oldest coffeehouse. Linda was formerly a teacher and worked at Dede Wallace Community Mental Health Center. Bob, also from C.T.S., worked at the state psychiatric hospital. Stephen and Dick were both from C.T.S. and worked at the Television and Radio Commission of the Methodist Church. Christine, a C.T.S. student, worked as cochaplain at the Presbyterian-Methodist Campus Center for Vanderbilt and Peabody universities. John was a law student at Vanderbilt. Paul joined us at Christmas when Mary decided to return to school to continue her seminary education, and he worked as the head carpenter at the State Historical Museum. Jan and Karen, both from C.T.S., had the dubious distinction of having more jobs for the first year than anyone else, the two of them frequently working together. Their longest employment was as members of the staff of the Tennessee Council on Human Relations. I spent the first part of the year working as a shipping clerk and the rest of the year at a local YMCA as youth program director.

Partly as a result of the seminary background of nine of the eleven of us, the institutional church and various forms of ministry were something that the group was quite aware of. This was not, however, carried on through full and regular church participation in Sunday morning services, as this generally did not speak to us of our own ministries which were primarily outside the church and in our jobs. Some of us attended church quite regularly and participated in church activities. Chris was one of the two ordained ministers in the group, and she was frequently involved in meetings across the country on the role of women in the church.

One way in which the church entered into the group as a whole was through the Constructive Theology course which we took with a seminary professor friend who came over to the house weekly. Out of this grew the personal theological statements of those who had been in seminary and a general theological awareness and unstated group theology. The latter was reflected in part by the fact that many in the group saw this experience, which started off as just one year away from school seeking clinical experience and seminary credit toward our degrees, as a form of mission or ministry. We wanted to explore group living and see if it was a viable form for individual or group ministry and to share our findings about this experience with others. This we did with friends, on television, before groups, and through writing. Also, the group talked many, many hours of a group ministry or project, such as starting a growth center or community learning center, or picking a neighborhood church to work with, or some social action or political project. This did not happen with the group as a whole participating, though individuals sometimes carried through these projects in their own ways.

What was it like to live at Covey House? Weekdays were spent at work. Weekday evenings were spent doing various things as individuals or as a group. Everyone in the house was single except my wife and me, and sometimes people would go out for a date or have someone over. There were occasional small social get-togethers where some went out to get a drink, to see a movie, or to drive around. Or people stayed at home either to work on a project, such as the garden, painting, making candles, carving, carpentry, reading, or just plain talk together. Our regular business meetings fell on Monday evenings, and we met for our theology class on Thursday evenings. Saturday and Sunday were often spent running errands and relaxing at home or away.

Covey House has meant a great deal to me. It was a place where I found support—support for me, for me as the person who I was and who I became. If I had questions or problems about my work or my personal life, I knew there were people around me who cared for me and were interested in me, and that I could always find someone to listen to me who would in turn share their ideas with me. At the same time I was criticized . . . but it was criticism that encouraged and enabled me to continually reexamine my work and my life and the way I related to the people and situations around me. There were different perspectives held by different people, and these different opinions were important to me. These same people offered me the privacy I sometimes needed as well.

To me, Covey House was in some ways like a family and a marriage. I felt there was the sort of love, sharing, and commitment that one may find in marriage, yet there was not total commitment. People were free to leave the commune if they wished, when they wished. Covey House has been one of the more meaningful experiences of my life; there I was able to be myself and be accepted as myself, although not everyone agreed with me or my behavior at all times. I have come to believe that communal living, as I experienced it, can be a very worthwhile way to live, not only for a year or two, though that can also be of value as it has been for me, but even for a lifetime. Communal living is not for everyone, but I feel everyone could and would learn from it—about themselves, about others, and about the world in which we live.

Epilogue

Covey House has continued since I was there in much the same ways as the first year, yet there have been changes as well. Several people have new and better jobs. The group is now in a new house, which was picked out by the group to be bought by a friend who is renting it to the group. Two of the individuals have bought 125 acres of relatively undeveloped land for which the remainder of the group is making monthly payments. Covey House had a party at Christmas time with over 150 guests—all kinds of people from all walks of life who are friends of the house and the people in it—which may reflect how widely Covey House is known in Nashville. The nine individuals currently living there have made a commitment to each other to maintain the community for several more years.

Suggestions For Digging Into The Issue

Discussion Questions

1. What would you consider the difference between a Christian commune and a secular commune? Did the commune depicted in this article qualify as a Christian one?

2. What were the common elements that made for success in this situation? Would the results have been different if some of the members had come from different religious backgrounds? if some of the members were from a variety of ethnic or racial backgrounds? if some of the members were drastically older or younger than these people?

3. This description of a commune has been called similar to "Ma Flanagan's Boarding House of 1890 as depicted in a B movie of the late forties." Do you agree? Is this experience more like a lark than an

alternate lifestyle? If so, what is the difference between a genuine lifestyle and the one described here?

4. "Communal living is not for everyone," writes the author. What kind of persons are best fitted for communal living? What kind are least fitted?

A Retreat or a Trip

Try organizing a retreat or short trip for your group on a communal basis. Instead of letting one leader or a committee parcel out the work and make decisions, let the entire group participate—or at least decide how things should be done. You can share much of the property, although as the case study indicates, individuals can still keep personal possessions. You may have to think before dividing up tasks on the basis of sex. After the experience, discuss whether the communal idea is a good one. It might also be worthwhile to talk about communal living as a style for expressing faith and love.

A Survey

Take a survey of your town or community to see what kinds of communes are going on. Some of these may be "semicommunes"—arrangements where couples or families share a house, but do not live together as a group. It might be possible to ask some members of these local communes to visit your youth group and talk about the commune as a lifestyle. Or you can visit them.

Additional Resources

Rental and/or sale prices of Additional Resource items are available from distributors listed at the back of the book. Books, many of which are in paperback, are generally available through any bookstore and/or local public libraries.

Feature Film

Alice's Restaurant (color, 111 min. UA 16). Experience in a commune.

Short Films

From Runaway to Hippie (b/w, 18 min. Association Films). NBC portrayal of teenage boys leaving home to find happiness via drugs on "hippie" communal farm.

A Circle of Love (color, 25 min. McGraw-Hill).

Children Adrift (b/w, 26 min. Mass Media). Child and grandfather share life together and realize how much another's humanity matters.

Family Life: A Kibbutz (color, 15 min. BFA). Living, working and growing up together in community.

The Hippie Temptation (color, 51 min. McGraw-Hill). Study of lifestyle and behavior of hippies in a San Francisco colony.

Tapes

The Green Revolution (50 min. Pacifica).

Communes (31 min. Pacifica #BC0021.14).

Masks and Fig Leaves (39 min. CSDI #512).

Simulations

Discovering Spiritual Values in Community (ten 2-hr. sessions, Human Development Institute).

Encounter Tapes for Personal Growth Groups (ten 1½-hr. sessions, 6–12 persons, Human Development Institute).

Books

The Joyful Community by B. Zablocki (Baltimore: Penguin Books).

The New Families: Youth, Communes and the Politics of Drugs by Ross V. Speck et al. (New York: Basic Books).

The Children of Change by Don Fabun (New York: Macmillan).

Getting Back Together: One Man's Odyssey to Explore the New Way in American Life (New York: Coward, McCann & Geoghegan).

A Study of Chinese Communes, 1965 by S. J. Curki (Cambridge, Mass.: Harvard Univ. Press).

Periodicals

"Vibes: Brotherhood of the Spirit Commune, Warwick, Mass., and the N.Y. Branch of the Fort Hill Community, Roxbury, Mass.," in The New Yorker, August 7, 1971.

Youth on the Move

BY MELANIE TURNER

Trekking across the country, sometimes at night, foraging for food and shelter, with one skimpy change of clothes and little notion where they're headed—to an older generation it might sound like a forced death march on Bataan, but to contemporary American youth it's Nirvana: the world on $5 a day or less.

Today, more than ever before, students are exploring the world around them by traveling, both in their own country and abroad. While economic uncertainties and dollar devaluations drain adult travel, nothing can stem the ever swelling tide of student wanderers. Cashing in on cheap charter flights and youth fare rates, they descend on European and American cities, beckoned by an international youth culture that promises good times, a kind of sophistication, and if they're lucky, some self-knowledge.

Nine-Year-Olds on the Grand Tour

Since the seventeenth century the necessary culmination of the education of wealthy, aristocratic Britons and Americans has been the so-called Grand Tour of the Continent, an initiation excursion on which the young traveler in question is expected to savor the delights of European culture. Originally the tour followed college graduation, and more recent American tradition sandwiched it between the junior and senior years of college. But during the past few years the nature of the tour, and indeed of all travel, has altered radically.

Travel is still one of the rites of passage to maturity, but low-cost trans-Atlantic transportation, the major travel expense, has given kids from all classes opportunities that once only the rich enjoyed. For the new generation of American youth, international adventure is becoming more of a commonplace than a luxury. And it is not just collegians who are taking off for parts unknown. Today increasing numbers of American high school students, study, do volunteer work, live with families, or tour abroad. For some junior high youth, international adventuring has even become a popular alternative to summer camp. In *Future Shock*, Alvin Toffler notes the tearful response of

Beth, a New York psychiatrist's daughter, who learned that her playmate had visited abroad: "I'm nine years old already and I've never been to Europe."

While these children of the jet age now have the means to indulge the wanderlust that previous generations could only feel, they are lured to travel for a variety of reasons. Some come to study. Others, driven by the scarcity of summer jobs, find it an inexpensive alternative to staying home. Despite the image of aimless flower child or drug freak, most are on rather serious quests. A growing curiosity about the world has led them to pursue fresh experience with a sense of discovery both of themselves and of the outside world. What seems to motivate a number of these young nomads is their search for something they can no longer find in modern urban America—an unharried, nonmaterialistic way of life.

Some of them, exactivists and veterans of the protest scenes of the sixties, display a certain apathy toward affairs of their country. Politically disillusioned and cynical about organized movements, most youth have, as a recent survey expressed it, given up the "action model" of behavior for the "self-development model." Much of their energy is now inwardly directed toward very personal goals of self-awareness and peace of mind. Seeking to know themselves and fleeing from middle-class America, they travel to "get their heads together." And exposing oneself to unfamiliar ways can generate a sense of vitality and awareness, an interest in life that can come when one's sensibilities are jolted through the experience of contrast and difference. For a surprising number the search for themselves does not end with the summer—it continues for a year or more. The value of travel experience for putting things in perspective is now so commonly accepted that an increasing number of colleges routinely grant a leave-of-absence to a student choosing to "drop out" for a year or two of travel.

Searching for That Free Lunch

For whatever reasons youthful vagabonds set out, they have evolved a lifestyle of their characteristic ways and means of travel. In Europe this style has created a totally new image of the American tourist abroad.

Donning the universal youth uniform of Levis, T-shirt, and sandals, U.S. youngsters merge with the international youth culture in such a way that language barriers seem almost nonexistent. The rapport is instantaneous as they participate in common rites of underground movies, rock music, drugs, and rap sessions. Indistinguishable from their European counterparts, they seem to have more in common with them than with adult Americans.

Shunning the middle-class values that no doubt helped finance their trip, these footloose travelers, once on foreign soil, adopt a compulsive thrift. Young people consistently avoid the displays of affluence that, to Europeans, characterized their chauvinistic, camera-toting elders, and they willingly forgo amenities that they might have demanded at home. Even the wealthiest Texas oilman's daughter, when traveling the student circuit, will spend extra hours scrounging for a room that is $1.50 instead of $2—only to pay for it by pulling out a wad of $100 travelers' checks.

Traveling light, usually with a change of clothing and a backpack, the economy-minded youth contingent follows the student grapevine, which can be counted on to inform the young traveler of bargains and scenes too current for guidebooks. The hordes of peripatetic youngsters that throng the squares and plazas of Europe's larger cities have forced local officials to provide inexpensive facilities. Amsterdam, whose Dam Platz is a proverbial student gathering place, has set aside parks for free overnight use, provided city-run cafes, and set up a Youth Advisory Service. And practically every student knows of the free food and beer that comes with a tour of the Heineken brewery. Copenhagen has prepared for its youth influx by erecting special campsites. A number of other cities have converted old factories for use as "crash pads," where wanderers can lay down a sleeping bag and share whatever food there is. A large number of American wanderers use the residences of their friends, or friends of friends, as stopping places in their travels around the country.

While swarms of summer expatriates can always be spotted mingling in London's Piccadilly Circus or basking in the sun on Rome's Spanish steps, it is not for this mob scene that most of them are there. For large numbers the major cities serve primarily as way stations—places to rest, pick up mail and money at American Express, and

swap travel lore with fellow itinerants. While they do not neglect the cities' historical attracions, many seek the regional flavor of out-of-the-way places to "get into the heads" of the natives. Unlike many of their elders who travel abroad, students generally do not try to impose American values on their foreign hosts. More often they seek as best they can to immerse themselves in the culture of another country. Interested in sharing a more total experience, they are eager to meet the people themselves on their own terms.

In recent years these roving ambassadors have changed their destinations as much as their style and mechanics of travel. In seeking new and unspoiled places, their excursions might have been more aptly labeled the "Grand De-tour." Turned off by the 36-countries-in-28-days package trip their parents quite likely took, these adventurers tend to spend more time in fewer countries in their impromptu ramblings. The certain inverted snob appeal accorded those who spend the least amount of money is also extended to those who haunt the most esoteric and isolated terrains.

How to Terrify Parents

For more and more students, Europe is becoming just a preliminary to the less-traveled realms of Asia, Africa, and Latin America. Some locales are attractive because of their political or ethnic significance—Egypt, Nigeria, Israel, Ireland, Vietnam. The Eastern bloc countries have a special appeal because of the implied risk and their active student movements. Prague, Budapest, and Warsaw are popular, and a side trip to Moscow, while perfectly harmless if one does not decide to photograph the missile sites, is, as one coed put it, "a sure-fire way to terrify your parents."

Asia is another region fast being canvassed by the new breed of Asian-studies students, guru-seeking meditators, and seasoned travelers in pursuit of unexplored territory. Japan is an ideal place to explore a totally different culture. It is not as physically demanding as more primitive areas, such as India, and the Japanese are eager to meet Americans. Unlike the Europeans, who have had their fill, the Japanese welcome visitors from a country they wish to know more about. Nearly all Japanese students speak some English, and a number plan to work in import companies and eventually come to the U.S. They are generous hosts and inveterate travelers themselves. While their homes are small and do not easily accommodate guests, Japanese students are usually willing to take along Americans as they explore their own country.

By Rail and Foot

Though the herd instinct of the young is evident in their common attire and their gravitation toward certain sanctioned watering holes, their individuality asserts itself in the different modes of transportation they choose.

The American hitchhiker can frequently count on friendly Europeans not only for a ride but usually for a meal and often for a night's lodging. It's also a great way to practice one's foreign language. Scott Jones, a veteran of some 7,000 miles of hitchhiking in this country, feels "hitching certainly beats flying if you want to see the land and talk with people. When I used to travel with my parents, I wanted to stop at the Civil War sites, but it was always rush, rush, rush to get somewhere, and we would always miss what we went through. You need to get a perspective of where you are."

One of the more popular and inexpensive means of moving around Europe is the Eurailpass—two months of unlimited second-class travel for $125. Trains in Japan are likewise inexpensive and efficient, but in the U.S. the closest comparison is the Greyhound bus.

Student chartered flights and night flights in Europe are cheap but unreliable, though extended waits are not necessarily a problem. Most young travelers are unconcerned about deadlines, schedules, or reservations. A typical scene occurred in Rome's international airport when a student flight to Athens and Tel Aviv, scheduled to depart at 6 A.M., did not leave the ground until 8 P.M. With none of the anxiety or consternation that might have been expected, these knights-of-the-road (or air) casually set up an instant commune-happening. Sleeping bags were rolled out; food, books, and magazines were exchanged; people mingled informally; even a multinational bridge game developed, complete with kibitzing by traveling Italian businessmen.

Other transportation alternatives are car or bike rentals or even leg power. In the Himalayas, where the trails are actually the communication networks between mountain villages, hiking is known as "trekking." An unusual coterie of international adventure-seekers trek the mountain sides around Katmandu, spending the nights in tiny huts and getting fed "all-you-can-eat" rice and vegetables for 35 cents. It is customary to travel without supplies in the Himalayas, since hospitality is readily available anywhere one may stop. Sharon Wolz, recently returned from a year of traveling throughout Asia, expressed a prevalent attitude: "The best things are always away from the tourist areas, seeing and feeling on your own."

Getting to Know the Natives

One of the better ways to get an understanding of another culture in a short period is to live as a part of a foreign family. Several programs offer this kind of experience. Other programs arrange volunteer or low-paying work in places ranging from a Swiss hospital to a French vineyard. A number of students also try kibbutzim.

Camping, popular with American travelers, attracts more converts every year. The camping explosion, however, has had some unpleasant fallout. Sites are frequently crowded and Barbara Moore, who spent three months camping in the U.S. and Canada, noted a growing hostility between the backpackers and those using tent campers and big trailers. Arriving equipped with their TVs and motorcycles, those towing trailers seem to some hikers more interested in avoiding motel costs than appreciating the return to nature.

In Europe youth hostels are still the most frequently sought lodging for the migratory student flock. Spartan in style and cheap in price, hostels provide an informal meeting ground with foreign counterparts. Visions of a communal sleep-in can be quickly discarded, for these establishments are carefully segregated by sex and stick to somewhat strict rules, including the practice of locking doors around eleven at night. Yet the ambience of the student-travel scene prevails, and hostels offer excellent opportunities to meet people, especially for those traveling alone. John and Kathy Morland inadvertently met in the shower of a Salzburg youth hostel (there was only one stall, and he thought it unoccupied) and married three years later.

Other good bets for cheap accommodations and student contacts are universities. Both European and American institutions often rent out their dormitory rooms to traveling students. And by frequenting university cafeterias and student haunts, one can get inexpensive fare and pick up tips from the campus bulletin boards.

The variety of tours taken each year by the student population seems infinite. A number are combination study-travel tours, ranging from intensive language study to a program in oceanography and ecology at the University of Aberdeen to courses in Mediterranean studies in Rhodes and Haifa. A majority of the organized "sight-seeing" tours, usually female-dominated, are well-chaperoned and provide more security for the apprehensive first-timer and his or her anxious parents. Certain savings also result from travel with a group, although this mode lacks the glamour and such benefits as independence and possible growth in self-confidence likely to be gained in a less-structured approach.

Any method of travel can be a new and exciting experience simply because it is different from staying at home. But the most meaningful experiences, in terms of growth in self-awareness and in personal development, are more likely to occur when the traveler sheds many of the habitual props of culture. In other words, the fewer friends one travels with, the more unfamiliar terrain one explores, and the more consciously open one is, the greater the chances for new insights.

When large groups travel together, they tend merely to transport their own community to a new locale. The individuals in this situation continue to be reinforced by familiar patterns of relationships and frames of reference. The security of the group usually does not allow for the healthy sense of uneasiness and alertness that one would experience alone as differences are perceived between the traveler and those around him or her. Groups traveling often seem more perceptive to the differences in physical things than in the people or ideas they encounter, and the individual response is often superseded by the group attitude.

When one is not sure who one is or where one is going, the unfettered experience of travel can put things in perspective. By temporarily dropping out, one can undergo an exhilarating sense of freedom—freedom from the responsibilities of a structured lifestyle and, more importantly, freedom to experience oneself and the world with a fresh vision. For the free and easy youthful travelers, where one is going is not as relevant as how one experiences where he or she is. Getting there —the existential experience of the lifestyle of student travel—is a large part of what the trip is all about.

Suggestions For Digging Into The Issue

Discussion Questions

1. Why do people travel? Does this generation of youth travel more than other generations? (Consult an over-thirty person to help answer this question.)

2. In what ways is the desire to travel compatible with Christian faith? Does it sometimes lead to irresponsibility and therefore immoral behavior?

3. What objections do parents and other adults sometimes have to individual travel by youth? How does a young person deal with these objections if he or she really wants to travel?

4. The kind of travel described in this article is usually not tied in with a moral or social goal, such as taking part in a work camp. When youth groups plan trips, ought they always to have a "useful" purpose in mind, or do you consider it okay to take a trip just for the sake of traveling?

Sharing Sessions

Invite parents whose sons or daughters have traveled to visit with the group and share their fears and hopes and whether these were soundly based. It might be possible to have the travelers themselves on hand, though it is likely they would still be away or would have grown up and moved off. There may be some travelers in your group or congregation. Invite them to share their experiences, particularly with respect to some of the issues raised in the article: is it true that youth are more concerned about the process of travel itself and not the destination? Is the danger of crime or accident negligible? Are most foreigners as friendly to Americans as the writer says?

True/False Test

Ask members of your group to respond to the following questions. Afterwards, discuss different views about the statements made here and what these statements say about the present obsession with travel.

	TRUE	FALSE
A. Most kids like to travel because even a middle-class life these days is boring.	____	____
B. The reason travel is fun is that you get out from under the eye of adult supervision.	____	____
C. Any girl going traveling by herself better learn how to defend herself first.	____	____
D. This travel business is strictly for rich, white kids; you don't see many blacks and Puerto Ricans hitchhiking across the country.	____	____
E. Travelers are more likely to fall under the influence of drugs than nontravelers.	____	____
F. This generation of youth likes travel because it is a generation that is more tolerant and understanding of different kinds of people than previous generations.	____	____

Additional Resources

Books listed (many are in paperback) are generally available from bookstores and/or local public libraries. Rental and/or sale prices of other Additional Resource items are available from distributors; their addresses are listed at the back of the book.

Feature Films

Easy Rider (color, 95 min. rbc Films). Youth on a journey to discover America.

Walkabout (b/w, 95 min. Fox). Study of contrasts between worlds of civilization and savagery.

Five Easy Pieces (color, 100 min. rbc Films). An adult dropout running from life.

Short Films

Hitchhiker: Why Young People Take to the Road (color, 30 min. Time-Life). Interviews with young hitchhikers and some of their experiences on the road.

Youth on the Road (color, 12 min. German Consulate General, free loan). Youth traveling in Germany to experience life.

Records

Bookends (Columbia #KCS 9529). Simon and Garfunkel sing "America" among other selections.

Parsley, Sage, Rosemary and Thyme (Columbia #LS 9363). Simon and Garfunkel sing "Homeward Bound" among other selections.

Books

Dreams from the Road by Brad Niles (Winona, Minn.: St. Mary's College Press). Personal reflections and photos of young man "on the road" concerned with the American scene.

Encyclopedia of World Travel (Garden City, N.Y.: Doubleday).

Going Light—With Backpack or Burro by D. R. Brower (New York: Sierra Club).

Traveling with Your Camera: Creative 35mm Photography by A. E. Woolley (Radnor, Pa.: Chilton Book Co.).

Thumb Tripping by Don Mitchell (Boston: Little, Brown). A former staff member of the American Baptist Convention tells about economical travel across the U.S.

Teen Age Summer Guide (Woodbury, N.Y.: Barron's Education Series).

Appalachian Hiker by Edward Garvey (Octon, Va.: Appalachian Books).

Invest Yourself: Involvement in Action—A Catalogue of Service Opportunities (475 Riverside Drive, New York, N.Y. 10027: Commission on Voluntary Service and Action).

Periodicals

G. Cravens, "Hitching Nowhere: The Aging Young on the Endless Road," in *Harpers*, September 1972.

"In Transit (Literally) Religious Bands from Semi-Communal State," in *Christianity Today*, April 1971.

"Making the Van Go," in *Time*, September 6, 1971.

International Christian Youth Exchange

ICYE sponsors exchange years for individuals (they typically live in homes of host families) and encourages encounter among persons of all convictions to further commitment to and responsibility for reconciliation, justice, and peace in the world. For information write to: U.S. Committee, International Christian Youth Exchange, 55 Liberty Street, New York, N.Y. 10005.

Chauvinism—The Way It Is in the Office

BY MICHAEL KORDA

Sexism At Work...

During a typical day, what are the relationships between male and female coworkers, and where does inequality occur?

9 A.M.

At this hour, everywhere you look women are striding briskly to work, weaving in and out of the traffic on bicycles, jaywalking across the bows of furiously thwarted taxi drivers.

Most of these women are striding toward their typewriters and yesterday's unfinished dictation, toward banking jobs where they count money rather than make it, toward work with no future except more of the same. Married or unmarried, ambitious or not, they are making their daily rendezvous with a world in which women are largely *tolerated* on the grounds that men can no more be expected to use a typewriter or answer the telephone than to wash socks or clean house.

For this, they have made excruciating arrangements with sitters to care for their children, strange and sometimes humiliating compromises with their husbands, or simply left behind them family, friends, safety, and comfort, to undergo the process of character-building (or destruction) that being a working woman in a man's world so often represents.

Women are fast becoming America's true proletarian class. It is women who find themselves doing the cooking after a hard day's work, who are shunted into "women's" jobs (by definition lower paid and static), who get harassed, patronized ("She's really good; I mean, she doesn't think like a woman. . . ."), saddled as if God's will with the everyday problem of children (teething, diapers, school grades, low-grade viruses—all the things men profess not to understand or to be able to cope with).

If they are married, they work mostly on sufferance. If they are unmarried, they bear the brunt of urban disintegration, praying their fillings will hold out because they can't afford dental bills and Blue Cross doesn't cover teeth, living in buildings that union workers have fled from, where security is a peephole, a police lock, a heavy chain, and a steel bar to wedge against the door. Or they accept the alternative: a dormitory life with three other girls in a "luxury" apartment where everyone sleeps on sofa beds, where someone else's wet pantyhose is always hanging in your face when

— 39 —

you take a bath, where you can't bring a man home without worrying about whether your roommate is out as she agreed to be or has reneged.

9:45 A.M.

The hallway of a large corporate office.

Leaning against the water cooler, two men—both minor executives—are nursing their cardboard cartons of coffee, discussing yesterday's ballgame, postponing for as long as possible the moment when work must finally be faced.

A vice president walks by and hears them talking about sports. Does he stop and send them to their desks? Does he frown? Probably not. Being a man, he is far more likely to pause on his way and join the conversation, anxious to prove that he, too, is "one of the boys."

Now let us assume that two women are standing by the water cooler discussing whatever you please: women's liberation, clothes, work. The vice president walks by, sees them, and moves off in a fury down the hall, cursing and wondering whether it is worth the trouble to complain—but to whom?—about all those bitches standing around gabbing when they should be working. "Don't they know this is an office?" he will ask, in the words of a million other men.

There is another aspect to this curious social phenomenon. Men are always given the benefit of the doubt, in that two men talking in the hall generally will be presumed to be discussing business matters until it has been proved otherwise, whereas women are "wasting time."

No man, I think, can really understand the ways in which women are made to feel guilty in the course of the working day. It is not just that they mostly have duller jobs than men, or make less money, or have fewer opportunities, all of which is true but can be explained or at any rate rationalized. It is that men find in women exactly those qualities they are afraid to admit to in themselves or, that lacking, they despise.

A man who is sloppy not only will expect his secretary to compensate for his sloppiness, but will inevitably suggest that her neatness and capacity for organization are proof of a tidy, and therefore limited, mind. His sloppiness, of course, is the sign of unfettered creativity, making her feel guilty for having exactly those abilities he lacks. The more successful she is at straightening the mess, the more she proves her inability to really succeed.

10:30 A.M.

The serious routine of the day has long since begun. For those women lucky enough to have jobs that are defined, that have a precise purpose and limits, their work is being done (or not being done) like anyone else's.

But this, of course, is the great dividing line. Men tend to have jobs that are quite easily defined. They know what they can be expected to do and what they aren't expected to do. Most women are not so lucky. They must simply take the work that is given them, either in the form of routine or in sporadic bursts, often without any explanation of why the work has to be done.

It is obvious that most women have begun—out of fear, guilt, or helplessness—by accepting the role of "go-fer" in the first stages of their working careers, partly because it's expected of them and partly because many of them have been brought up to feel that this kind of subservience is natural to them. Having failed to define their jobs at the beginning, they can do so later only by an extreme effort of will and courage, which as likely as not will be misconstrued as "temperament."

Noon

An executive's secretary goes out to the receptionist's desk to bring in a young man—younger than she is—to be interviewed for a job. As she shows him into the office, her boss says cheerily, "Hey, June, write that letter for me, okay? Tell him no, but make it nice, and I'll sign it after lunch. Oh, and make me a reservation for two at 12:30, usual table. . . ."

A reservation for a lunch with this bright young man just down from Harvard who isn't sure he wants to go into business, but is undeniably smart. So June, who came down from Radcliffe with a B.A. and had to take a typing test before being hired as a secretary-assistant, books a table for the young man from Harvard, who has compromised his integrity to the extent of wearing a suit and a tie reluctantly knotted on an old work shirt. June knows he will be told across the breadsticks:

"The thing is, we're looking for talent, for people who will stay, who will bring something special to us. You'd start as my assistant, but I'm easy to work with, and I want you to do your own thing, to find your feet as quickly as possible, to contribute. Dress the way you want, tell us what we're doing wrong.

"We'll learn some things from you; you'll learn from us. Can you start at $7,500 a year? I know it's low, but we'll make it up to you later if it works out."

... Whereas she was told (no lunch, but an office interview):

"What I'm looking for is someone who can really work for me, someone I can rely on. It's very important that I get my messages, and there's a lot of routine work that has to be done. Anyway, I like you, and if you want the job, it's yours, assuming your typing is okay. I can start you at $110, but we can get you $120 at the end of the year, if it works out. And of course you get Blue Cross and all that. . . ."

June watches the two men go off to lunch, knowing she will soon have to teach yet another young man the ropes, show him how to make out the expense account she doesn't have, watch him sit in on meetings that she can't go to.

It's not that men are brighter or even better trained. More success oriented, maybe, but the main thing, June knows, as she unwraps her sandwich, is that they get a head start.

They begin their careers generally at exactly the point most young women spend years trying to reach. They don't have to begin as secretaries, to survive the long period of initiation in which a woman is valued not just for what she does, but for those negative qualities her role so often requires: lack of independent judgment, absence of initiative, fear of displaying ambition.

Do men realize that most young women are being asked to not compete by the very nature of their jobs, that it takes extraordinary strength and guile to break out of this trap?

Michael Korda's book *Male Chauvinism—How It Works* was published by Random House in 1973. This article, an excerpt from his book, appeared in a prepublication seres in the *Chicago Tribune*, beginning on June 17, 1973. It is reprinted here by permission.

Suggestions For Digging Into The Issue

Discussion Questions

1. What is the real meaning of *chauvinism* and why do you think it exists? Do you believe that chauvinism is not as bad as some say it is?

2. Is it true that men can probably not understand the subtle ways in which women are discriminated against? Can the gap between the sexes be bridged by an understanding heart?

3. To what extent is the attitude that women are inferior rooted in the Bible and religion? Given this religious sanction for male superiority, how does a faithful Christian apply religious faith to the issue of freedom for women?

4. What advice do you have for women who want to change things and correct some of the injustices relating to the treatment and status of women?

Create a Model

The usual model for male-female relationships is one with the male in control and the female subordinate to him. See how many other models you can conceive that might be healthy for men-women relations. Then you might try out this model (which could be described in words or even drawn in a diagram) in a role play or simulation.

Interview

Use a tape recorder to interview several men and women in an "on the street" setting to find out their views on the feminist movement. You will probably get more from the persons interviewed if you ask rather specific questions, but ask them over and over to different persons. Such a procedure elicits more direct answers and enables the listener to compare the responses. Play back the tape for a larger group. The group can then go on to discuss issues related to chauvinism and the feminist movement.

Action on Legislation

Find out the status of the proposed Equal Rights Amendment to the U.S. Constitution in your state. If the amendment has not been passed, consider some ways of making contact with your local state representative or senator on the issue: writing a letter, making a personal visit, or joining with community organizations in exerting influence. If the ERA has already been voted on, find out from the League of Women Voters, Church Women United, the local chapter of the National Organization for Women (NOW), or similar groups what state and local laws allow or do not permit in the area of women's rights.

Very often legislation is pending even though the ERA has been disposed of.

Additional Resources

Rental and/or sale prices of Additional Resource items are available from distributors listed at the back of the book. Books, many of which are in paperback, are generally available through any bookstore and/or local public libraries.

Feature Films

Three Lives (color, 70 min. Impact). Kate Millet's all-female-made film on what it is to be a woman.

Ramparts of Clay (subtitles, color, 85 min. Cinema 5). Drama of one woman's inability to accept subservient role.

Short Films

Abortion: Public Issue or Private Matter? (color, 25 min. NBC). Whose decision is abortion?

Take This Woman (color, 25 min. NBC). Women's employment used to full potential?

The Black Woman (b/w, 52 min. Indiana Univ.). Her role in American society.

Women Talking (b/w, 80 min. Impact). Conversations with leading personalities of the women's liberation movement.

Filmstrips

Women: The Forgotten Majority (2 parts, color, Denoyer-Geppert).

The Silenced Majority: A Woman's Liberation Multi Media Kit (5 parts, color, Media Plus).

The Changing Role of Women (2 parts, color, Scott Education).

Tapes

Toward a Neuter Gender (28 min. CSDI #189).

The New Woman (46 min. Center for Cassette Studies).

Training the Woman to Know Her Place (60 min. Pacifica #BC0426).

All Issues Are Women's Issues (39 min. Pacifica #BC0719).

The Oppression of Women, The Pill, and The Coed—Four Brief Talks (four tapes, each approx. 15 min. Pacifica #s AP1166.01 through AP1166.04).

Books

Liberation Now ed. Deborah Balco (New York: Dell).

Understanding Women's Liberation by Edythe Cudlipp (New York: Warner Paperback Library).

The New Woman: A Motive Anthology of Women's Liberation by Joanne Cooke (New York: Fawcett).

Roles Women Play: Readings Toward Women's Liberation ed. M. Garskof (Monterey, Calif.: Brooks-Cole).

Up Against the Wall, Mother—A Women's Liberation Reader by Elsie Adams (New York: Macmillan).

The Feminine Mystique by Betty Friedan (New York: Dell).

Periodicals

P. F. Palmer, "Christian Breakthru in Women's Lib," in *America*, June 19, 1971.

J. D. Floerke, "Poetry, Sex, and Women's Rights," in *Christian Century*, June 16, 1971.

E. Woo, "Theology Confronts Women's Liberation," in *America*, March 13, 1971.

S. D. Collins, "Women and the Church: Poor Psychology, Worse Theology," in *Christian Century*, February 17, 1971.

Ms. (annual subscription $9; address: Ms. Magazine, Subscription Department, 123 Garden Street, Marion, Ohio 43302).

Young and Gay and Alone

BY MICHAEL AUSTIN

Me—a homosexual? For years I struggled with that question. Whenever I got hold of a book on sexuality I spirited it away to my room and read the chapter on homosexuality first. Was that me? No, of course not—the descriptions of overdomineering mothers and weak-willed fathers, the terminology of sickness and deviance made no sense in my own life. But . . . ? Little things still made me wonder, however dimly. My friends said they liked the pictures of girls in *Playboy,* but I was more interested in the pictures of men modeling clothes. I always wondered whether boys really meant it when they admired a girl's legs and whistled while I felt nothing, but I (quite unconnectedly in my mind) looked whenever I could at guys' legs and chests. I formed deep friendships with other boys that meant something more to me than they were "supposed" to. Often my sexual fantasies concentrated more on the male than female—and just as often that frightened me. And once in junior high school, before I understood I should avoid it, I had a homosexual experience with a friend I spent the night with.

Did these feelings make me a homosexual? I dealt with that nagging question in a number of ways. The textbook description certainly did not fit my sensitive, well-adjusted parents and family, and its general overtones reinforced my fears. Sometimes I just ignored my feelings and tried to convince myself that my real love for girls precluded love for boys. Still, rarely did it occur to me to kiss a girl at the end of a date (I just wasn't interested), and my friendships with guys were ever deepening. After a surge of questioning while a sophomore in high school, I assured myself that it was only a passing phase and would soon disappear. Two years later it was difficult to use the same concept. None of the rationales held up. Although I could intellectually accept homosexuality as a viable lifestyle and gay people as real people, homosexuality was so alien from my idea of what I was *supposed* to be that it became a threat when it got too close.

These quesions continued to grow while I led what appeared to be a regular heterosexual life. Although I stopped my never frequent dating in the middle of my junior year, I developed some deep friendships with a few girls and always felt very comfortable with them. I hugged and kissed girls because I loved them, but I did not touch boys I loved because I feared that would scare them off. I thought seriously about my relationships with girls, and even had a few "man-to-man" talks with friends about them. Last year I went to college, studied, worked in a dining hall, saw some movies, made some friends. The Gay Alliance dance posters intrigued me, but I dared not attend them—especially after my roommates mocked the very notion. I checked the college's library (one of the best), and found nothing helpful about homosexuality. Most of my questioning was submerged as I was pulled deeper and deeper into academia's demands, but I continued to enjoy boys' bodies and developed a couple of significant relationships with guys. It was easy at first to avoid the questions, and I did so gratefully. There were times during the second semester, however, when it became apparent to me that I could no longer deny my suspicions. In long walks I examined what was going on in my head: one part of me shouted that this is who you are, while another cried that it could not be so.

It was a very lonely time in this respect, as it had always been. I had heard enough cruel jokes about fags and had sensed such powerful hostility that I knew better than to express my feelings and doubts openly. While I had kept a journal for three years, I never mentioned that one most important question. A journal entry would give it too much credibility—and might be seen by someone. I could not talk with my parents, who might worry that "the blame" was theirs. How could I share my feelings with a close friend and not tell him I loved him—and thus perhaps scare him away? I did not want to discuss it with someone who didn't know me just because he or she would NOT know me and would not really be able to understand who I was. So I kept it all inside me. It was hardly an obsession since many activities and other sorts of questioning took most of my attention—but it was always there.

All of this culminated just a few months ago, near the end of my first year in college. A thirty-year-old friend who teaches at my old high school had to do some research so she came to visit me and our library for a weekend. We first met when she helped with my church's youth group four years ago and have become very close since then. During those years our relationship has shifted from a friendly student and teacher to loving, open, and equal friends. The week before she came was a particular crisis week for me, and I finally decided to somehow squarely face and deal with my questions. So I was glad when she came, but doubted I would share my inner turmoil with her. She started the first night's conversation, and explained how stormy the last weeks had been for her as she and her lover dealt with some serious problems. I sat amazed. Her housemate, my friend, was her lover. She was gay, and I had never even suspected it. Although I had always been aware of their tremendous love and openness, my vision of homosexuality was so sex-oriented that their relationship had never occurred to me. When she ticked off a list of people I knew in the high school and city who were gay, I stopped her to whisper (my roommates, after all, were in the next room) that I, too, might be gay. Stunned, happy, affirming, the two of us, two intimate friends who had never suspected each other's sexual direction, shared our lives. We talked long into the night, and that has made all the difference in my life.

I am gay. I can say that now, and it does not scare me. Rather, it opens up all kinds of possibilities that I find very attractive and exciting. That I am gay means to me that I can love another human being who is also male, that I can become a more whole person. My love for other men is a love of tenderness, concern, and commitment as well as sex. I care very deeply for some people, feel comfortable and celebrative with them, and enjoy their bodies. The feelings I have had for years just have a name now, but that name symbolizes a recognition, acceptance, and affirmation of my nature. I used to shy away from the idea of love. "Friendship" is an easier term to use for guys. But I realize now that it is love that I feel. And it feels very very good to be able to say I love, to not worry when I hug, touch, care. The word *gay*, the fact that I love some guys, does not at all preclude my very real love for some girls, just as my acknowledged love for girls had not limited me before. In many ways I feel free for the first time, free to be who I am.

These are good words, good feelings. But where am I right now? I'm still pretty much alone, in a numerical sense, as very few people know that I am gay. But the terrible aloneness of loneliness is gone now. I have a few close older friends with whom I can talk and who have given me some good books to read. I have done a lot of reading and thinking and recollecting, and I look forward to the next academic year when I will not fear to attend gay dances or political meetings. I am, most importantly, in contact with a very important part of myself for the first time in many troubled years. Still, I am not at all sure how to relate as gay to the heterosexual world. I have not told my parents, but surely will after I've explored the gay world some more. I'll have a chance next year to meet some more people who are acknowledgedly gay, and that will be good, and I'll probably talk to some of my closest friends at school. I have a good sense of who I am, and think they will accept that. It is much more difficult to hate fags when you learn that your best friend is one. But the larger world does not know me at all now—would they reject me as homosexual before they had a chance to know me as me? Would you?

I have agreed to write this article under a pseudonym because I want to share with you some of the things that are going on in the head of a young person you know. Statistics indicate that in an average size youth group at least one person will be gay. If my experience is at all typical, and it surely is, you may well know this person intimately. The girl you know and love—who dates boys, is on the tennis team, or edits the school newspaper, who questions her church's religion or plans to go into the ministry—may well be in the midst of some real turmoil as she tries to understand and deal with her true sexuality. It is a very lonely process. It can be a very scary one.

It may be that you can do nothing directly to help that young person. But while the person may never seek counseling from you, there are some things you can do to ease her or his problems. Educate yourself about sexuality and especially homosexuality. Learn more about what it's like to grow up gay, the legal status of homosexuals, and the problems we face. A warning: much of the available literature about homosexuality has been written by people who have a lot of deepdown anxieties to work out and/or by psychiatrists who generalize about all homosexuals on the basis of their experiences with the sick ones they meet professionally. There is, fortunately, a growing body of good literature. *Gay Crusaders* by Kay Tobin and Randy Wicker (New York: Warner Paperback Library, 1972—$1.25) is a must as far as I'm concerned. Other good books include George H. Weinberg's *Society and the Healthy Homosexual* (New York: St. Martin's Press, 1972), *Lesbian/Woman* by Del Martin and Phyllis Lyon (San Francisco: Glide Publications, 1972), and *I Have More Fun with You Than Anybody* by Lige Clarke and Jack Nichols (New York: St. Martin's Press, 1972). The most complete listing of available publications is *A Gay Bibliography: Brief List of Materials on Homosexuality*, developed by the Task Force on Gay Liberation, Social Responsibilities Round Table, American Library Association. Request a free copy (enclose stamped reply envelope) by writing to Barbara Gittings, Coordinator, Social Responsibilities Round Table, American Library Association, P.O. Box 2383, Philadelphia, Pa. 19103.

Read these books thoughtfully—but don't keep them to yourself! Get them into the public library, your church's collecion and your own bookshelf. Be sure everyone knows they are available. Perhaps no one will ask you directly for a book, but you can be sure they will be read.

Be sensitive in your attitudes about sexuality. When you express through your actions (and to a lesser extent your words) your concern for human liberation from dehumanizing roles, your openness to a variety of lifestyles, the questioning young person will feel that support. Most of the world tells the confused young person he or she is evil for even wondering seriously about his or her sexuality. You can help counterbalance that

tremendous, senseless force. Or at the other extreme, the next time you're about to call someone a dirty faggot, remember there's a fair chance you are speaking to (and damning and alienating) someone who is gay. I can say from experience that it happens all the time.

You cannot stop at providing resources and demonstrating attitudinal support. Work wherever you can to end the institutional oppression of gay people. Sodomy is against the law in most states; because of their sensitive legal situation gay bars are largely controlled by the underworld syndicates and entrapments are not uncommon. The laws have got to be changed: twenty million Americans cannot be labeled criminals because they love. The church has always been one of the strongest institutions downing gays, and if you work to change its repressive stands you will help change the laws and people's attitudes in the process.

Be informed about homosexuality and enable others to find information, be sensitive to the dilemmas young people face and your own attitudes toward sexuality, work to end the oppression of people. You will free yourself, and you may help someone you know who has the feelings I had a year ago to become free, to get in touch with him- or herself.

And, finally, a note to any of my fellow young homosexuals who read this: Gay is good. Don't fight it.

Suggestions For Digging Into The Issue

Discussion Questions

1. What is a gay lifestyle? Can a person be gay without living entirely within a gay style?

2. What derogatory names are often used for homosexuals of either sex? How do you think a Christian ought to respond when jokes are told at the expense of homosexuals?

3. Is it immoral from a Christian point of view to be gay? Why or why not?

4. Compare the treatment of gays with the treatment accorded minorities. In comparison, do gays seem repressed? What can be done to see that gays are treated with respect and given nondiscriminatory treatment under the law?

Panel or Symposium

Set up a panel or symposium on the subject, "A Gay Lifestyle Is a Human Lifestyle." You might ask such participants as a gay person, persons sympathetic to the feminist movement, a clergyman, and a "straight" married person.

Use Local Resources

Make contact with local gay organizations in your community. There may be a Gay Activist Alliance or a Gay Liberation Front in your city or community. Call and ask if there are speakers who can represent the organization at sessions of your local youth group. Check on dances, picnics, and other activities that are sponsored by gay organizations and are open to the public. Talk about taking part in some of these activities with the aim of getting to know gays as gays and understanding them on a person-to-person basis.

Discuss Sexist Images

A leader can initiate a discussion on distorted, sexist ideas of the image of God.

• Let the leader quite naturally and unobtrusively engage in some normal touching action with a person of the same sex in the group (shake hands, admire a piece of clothing or jewelry, pat on the shoulder, etc.). Then, equally unobtrusively and with a deadpan face, the leader can turn to the group and say "Did you know that _____ and I were having a homosexual relationship?" There will normally be considerable response from the group, and the leader should encourage persons to deal openly with sexuality, steering the discussion around to the understanding that all human relationships have a sexual component, precisely because we are all sexual beings. When this insight is out in the open, the leader may then engage in another action similar to the one that started the discussion, but this time with a person of the opposite sex. The leader may then look at the group and ask, "Now what kind of relationship were _____ and I having?" Most will respond, "Heterosexual." The leader will say, "Oh, no, ours was a divine relationship." The response will often be puzzled frowns. After some discussion, the leader can admit, perhaps reluctantly, that it was a heterosexual relationship and then point out that the previous homosexual relationship was also divine.

• At this point, ask a member of the group to read aloud Genesis 1:26–31. Make sure that members of the group clearly understand that our maleness and femaleness are constituents of the image of God that we bear. Then ask the group to consider God, and images of God: the stereotyped old man with a long white beard, the man upstairs, portrayals of God in human form. Be especially encouraging to any young women who want to talk about sexism in religion. Your group should focus on destroying sexist or other distorted ideas of the image of God.

• Then have someone read Ephesians 5:21–33 aloud. Follow with a discussion. Let the women, especially, be free in discussing what some would consider the sexism apparent in the passage. Then steer the discussion around to human relationships—male/female, male/male, and female/female as the image of God.

Additional Resources

Books listed (many are in paperback) are generally available from bookstores and/or local public libraries. Rental and/or sale prices of other Additional Resource items are available from distributors; their addresses are listed at the back of the book.

Feature Films

Sunday, Bloody Sunday (color, 110 min. UA 16). A man and a woman both in love with the same man.

The Silence (subtitles, b/w, 95 min. Janus).

The Killing of Sister George (color, 138 min. Films Inc.). A film about what two lonely, frustrated lesbians do.

Short Films

The Homosexuals (b/w, 47 min. UCC Office for Audio-Visuals; also Mass Media). The CBS News exploration of homosexuality.

Homosexuality in Men and Women (b/w, 60 min. Indiana Univ.). Helpful in fostering understanding of homosexuality.

Tapes

The Homosexuals and Society (53 min. Center for Cassette Studies).

How Good Is Gay? (23 min. CSDI #585).

The Lesbians (50 min. Pacifica #ALW1555).

On Being Gay (64 min. Pacifica #XX0046).

Aspects of Homosexuality Among Transvestites (26 min. Pacifica #AS1282).

The Contemporary Lesbian: Beyond Stereotypes (87 min. Pacifica #BC0448).

Transparency

The "Homosexual" Style of Development (Creative Visuals).

Television

That Certain Summer (CBS-TV Special, 1972).

Books

The Gay Militants by Donn Teal (New York: Stein and Day).

Sexuality and Homosexuality: A New View by Arno Karen (New York: W. W. Norton).

Homosexuality by Merle Miller (New York: Random House).

The Gay World: Male Homosexuality and the Social Creation of Evil by Martin Hoffman (New York: Basic Books).

Periodicals

The Furies (annual subscription $5; address: *The Furies*, Subscription Department, 8843 S.E. Station, Washington, D.C. 20003). Lesbian feminist newspaper.

Ain't I A Woman? (annual subscription $5; address: *Ain't I A Woman?*, P.O. Box 1169, Iowa City, Iowa 52240). Lesbian feminist newspaper.

Trends, July–August 1973— entire issue devoted to homosexuality. Beginning with a biblical perspective in the introduction, the articles include: "The Church and the Homosexual" and "The Mission of the Gay Church," and there is a list of additional resources and organizations. (*Trends* is published bimonthly by the Program Agency of The United Presbyterian Church in the United States of America as a resource for study by older youth and adults. Single copies are $1 each; three or more copies to one address are 80¢ each. Write: *Trends*, 723 Witherspoon Building, Philadelphia, Pa. 19107.)

Organizations

The Glide Foundation
330 Ellis St.
San Francisco, Calif. 94102

The Council on Religion and the Homosexual
(same address as Glide Foundation)

Future Shock in Marriage?

BY ARTHUR C. TENNIES

The women's liberation movement has made an old question—the roles of men and women in society—an issue of major concern. The marriage relationship is particularly crucial.

The women's liberation movement could make more common a pattern that now exists only rarely—that of the wife as the career pursuer and the husband as the helpmate. While this will seem to many to be a radical departure, it can be seen as part of a long-range trend. The traditional pattern of the husband as career pursuer and the wife as helpmate has become much less common, even though many people still think of this as the normal pattern. But, in fact, the pattern of husband and wife as partners has become more and more popular and common.

In this pattern both pursue careers and both share in the care of the home and family, and decisions about the future are made in light of both careers. The long-range trend would indicate that the traditional pattern will continue to decrease, the partner pattern, or some variation of it, will be the most common, and the wife as the career pursuer and the husband the helpmate will establish itself as an accepted pattern.

Queen and Consort

In this pattern the wife is the central figure in the family. Family life is oriented to her career. The husband has the major responsibility for the home and the children, the wife has the responsibility for the financial support of the family.

This is not an unknown pattern. Even though an English queen and her husband would not fit this pattern exactly, the same underlying concept is present: The wife is the career pursuer and the husband adjusts his life to facilitate her pursuit of a career. There has been a tendency for years for this pattern to emerge—particularly in entertainment and literary fields, as well as some professional and business careers.

Right now in our society, most people would view this pattern as abnormal. Some would probably view it as almost immoral, contrary to the laws of nature. Because of the role images in our society, how people ought to act or live in a given situation, it would be almost impossible for many men to function in this pattern.

Where such a pattern has tended to emerge naturally, such as in the marriage of a famous actress and a husband not so gifted, such marriages have tended to be very unstable and the husbands have felt that their status as men has been destroyed or seriously impaired. For these men the idea of being known as someone's husband is not tolerable. Society has tended to view such men as peculiar or lacking.

Unfair Choice

Society's view of such a pattern is irrational. It is obvious that only a small percentage of people can be famous, or geniuses, or eminent in professions. It does not condemn the wife of a genius because she is not a genius, or the wife of a famous painter because she cannot paint. Why should it condemn a man because his achievements in these terms are not up to his wife's? Such a view also is threatening to a woman who, because of luck or ability, achieves greater public prominence than her husband, because she may have to choose between her career and her marriage.

A strong case can be made for the pattern of the career wife and the helpmate husband as a valid, useful, and meaningful one. Just as the pursuit of some careers by men can best be facilitated by wives who are helpmates, so the pursuit of the same or similar careers by women could best be facilitated by husbands who are helpmates.

Because in this pattern the wife is the predominant partner, how can it be meaningful to the man? Just as in the pattern of the husband as career pursuer and the wife as helpmate, the organizing of the marital relationship around the career pursuit of the wife tends to reduce the possibilities for conflict and friction. Just as the wife can find meaning in supporting her husband in the pursuit of his career, so in this pattern the husband can find meaning by supporting his wife in the pursuit of her career. The sense of participation in a shared task—the wife's career—can be meaningful to both.

Management Expertise

The husband's possibilities in such a lifestyle are unlimited. For instance, if there are children, why should not the husband find this a challenging, demanding, and rewarding experience? There is just as much demand for knowledge and expertise as in any other job. Why should this be seen as any less of a career than school teaching?

The management of the household and its finances for maximum efficiency in a complicated economy requires a great deal of expertise. The husband who does this at all well uses as much of his capacity and demonstrates as much capability as he would in many income-producing jobs.

A man in this pattern does not have to limit himself to the household. He can develop a variety of interests. He can participate in political and church organizations. Our society depends on volunteers to perform a great variety of necessary or useful tasks, and it is possible for a man in this pattern to be involved in activities that are personally meaningful, require the development of expertise, and make a contribution to society.

A man can receive a great deal of meaning and satisfaction from the contributions that he makes to his wife's career by his support and companionship. He can share in her success. Many men, especially in positions of great pressure, have been able to function effectively only because of their wives. The reverse would be true for many women pursuing careers.

No Automatic Answer

If life is to be satisfying, one needs to experience a sense of meaning and self-fulfillment. How to achieve these is one of the most difficult and complex problems in our society. It seems to be clear from studies made of people and their jobs that having an income-producing job is not an automatic answer. The man living out this pattern is probably as free and has as much possibility of achieving these as in any other pattern. With the variety of labor-saving devices, housework probably introduces no more drudgery in this pattern than a man would find in most income-producing jobs. To point out these things is not to imply that every man ought to be able to find satisfaction in this pattern, but only to stress that the possibility is there, that such a pattern can provide a husband an opportunity to develop his abilities to the fullest.

There is a definite need for this pattern. For instance, an increasing number of women are seeking careers in politics, and this is good. Women have a great deal to contribute to the political process. Our country someday will have a woman President, and such a development won't come too soon; the British had their first ruling queen more than 400 years ago, and at that time the monarch ran the show. And in politics as in other careers, many women will require husbands who are supportive.

Many people will debate the question of which marriage pattern is the best on the basis of which pattern is the *right* one and, therefore, which one society should adopt. If one takes seriously the needs and rights of people, a debate on that basis is irrelevant—actually harmful. The real goal of society, true liberation, should be the freedom for each husband and wife to develop the most meaningful pattern. People are different. Any attempt to superimpose one pattern on all people may liberate a few, but will enslave the many. It would seem, then, the pursuit of freedom for all requires the development of a society in which there is much greater room for and acceptance of diversity.

The Rev. Arthur C. Tennies is director of church planning and research for the New York State Council of Churches and an associate on the staff of the United Presbyterian Board of National Missions. His article appeared originally in *The National Observer*, June 30, 1973, and is reprinted here by permission.

Suggestions For Digging Into The Issue

Discussion Questions

1. Do you understand the writer to be serious or writing with tongue in cheek? How do you react to the statement that "volunteers are needed, etc."?

2. Is there anything wrong with the traditional roles of husband and wife as long as they feel happy about it? What is the meaning of passages like Ephesians 5:22–23, I Corinthians 7:1–4, 39; 11:3, 11–12?

3. What can be said to the argument that the Bible speaks of wives being obedient to their husbands?

4. Is it possible to have a successful marriage if *neither* partner likes to work under any circumstances?

5. Do young people today seem to be more tolerant of differing styles of marriage? Why is this (your answer) true?

Resource Persons

Ask two or three young married couples to share with the group their approach to roles in marriage. The more diversity the better the discussion is likely to be.

Write a Contract

Draw up a model marriage contract or marriage service in which the rights and responsibilities of both partners would be spelled out.

Take a Survey

Survey several couples known to members of the group to find out how widely varying is the practice of making a strict "division of labor" or the practice of role reversal.

Additional Resources

Books, many of which are in paperback, are generally available through any bookstore and/or local public libraries. Rental and/or sale prices of other Additional Resource items are available from distributors listed at the back of the book.

Short Film

George & Betty: Career Versus Marriage (color, 10 min. Henk Newenhouse). A consideration of switched family roles.

Tape

The Transitional Family (14 min. CSDI #4910).

Books

Marriage: An Examination of the Man-Woman Relationship (New York: John Wiley & Sons).

Family in Transition: Rethinking Marriage, Sexuality, Child Rearing, and Family Organization by A.S. Skolnick (Boston: Little, Brown).

Without a Wedding Ring: Casework with Unmarried Parents by J. Pochin (New York: Schocken).

Periodicals

B. Longwood, "One Family's Flight from Middle Class America," in *Today's Health,* August 1972.

C. Dowling, "What Will Happen to the Children?" in *Saturday Review,* October 14, 1972.

M. Seligsor, "New Wedding," excerpt from *The Eternal Bliss Machine* by M. Seligsor, in *Saturday Review,* March 8, 1973.

D. Reuben, "Alternatives to Marriage," in *McCalls,* February 1972.

"New Marriage Style," in *Time,* March 20, 1972.

P. Coffin, ed., "Marriage Experiments," in *Life,* April 28, 1972.

"Swapping Family Roles: Role-Swapping Experiment by Couples in Norway," in *Time,* November 22, 1971.

NOTE: Most of the Additional Resources for "Chauvinism—The Way It Is in the Office" may also be appropriately used with this article.

Black Consciousness—
An Interview with C. Eric Lincoln

BY CHARLES E. COLE

For almost two decades Dr. C. Eric Lincoln has contributed to the understanding of issues in the sociology of religion, especially of the contributions and the role of blacks in America. His book *The Black Muslims in America,* originally published in 1961 (revised and updated in 1973), marked one of the first efforts on the part of a serious thinker to take account of the rising tide of black nationalism. He has since written many books, including *My Face Is Black* and *The Negro Pilgrimage in America.* In addition, he is the editor of the C. Eric Lincoln Series, a projected twenty volumes on black religion. Works already published in the series include *A Black Theology of Liberation* by James H. Cone; *Black Preaching* by Henry Mitchell; *Black Religion and Black Radicalism* by Gayraud Wilmore; *Black Sects and Cults* by Joseph Washington, Jr.; *Is God a White Racist?* by William Jones, and *Soul Force* by Lionel Barrett.

Dr. Lincoln is now chairman of the Department of Religious and Philosophical Studies at Fisk University. His two latest books, *The Black Church Since Frazier* and *The Black Experience in Religion,* were published in 1973 and 1974, respectively.

Q: Is there such a thing as black style, and what does that term mean to you?

LINCOLN: I think very definitely there is something that could be identified as black style. What it implies is that there is a certain way of looking at things, a certain way of behavior that reflects what one might call the subculture of BlackAmerica. It is perspective and it is response, and this might include the projection or perceived identity through styles of dress and adornment, sports or leisure-time activities, religious preference, choice of food, etc. It is a matter of a peculiar ethnic and cultural identification, understood or assumed in contrast to the prevailing styles of behavior.

Q: Columnist Carl Rowan has written that the emphasis on black style detracts from more important issues. Do you agree with his criticism?

LINCOLN: I think my good friend Carl Rowan is perhaps a little bit less secure in such matters than some others. There is a school of thought, as you know, which insists that the best thing for black people to do is to be as nearly like white people as possible. Perhaps Carl subscribes to this ideology. I do not. From my perspective, the black experience is in some important details different from the white experience, and I believe that when people project themselves *qua* themselves, rather than in terms of the signals received from their reference groups, their behavior is more authentic and relaxed. By "authentic" I mean behavior reflective of one's own experiences and the insights and values those experiences have produced. This is not to say that black people and white people never have common experiences. They do, and with increasing frequency. This is to say, though, that the peculiar history which describes the separate existence of Blacks and Whites in this country has produced lifestyles and patterns of behavior which are divergent or which tend to be distinctive at some points. There is no judgment implied in this recognition of difference. Rather, I consider it an unmisktakable sign of maturity when people are able to find value and satisfaction in themselves and their distinctive contributions to a common culture without sacrificing perspective and appreciation for others and their contributions.

Q: *By "black experience" in this country, you are referring to slavery?*

LINCOLN: Slavery is one aspect of an experience that is so much richer and broader than that alone. The black experience, as you know, did not begin with slavery or with the English in America. True, Blacks were brought to this country involuntarily, and the ongoing history of the African people was affected in a significant but temporary way by that fact. There developed a disjunction between the cultures of the Africans and the African diaspora* that was far more pronounced than the discontinuity between the prevailing American culture and the European culture from which it derived. But more than that, the total circumstances under which Blacks came to be Americans were so very different from those under which Whites came to that status that the cultural development of the black man was quite often peculiar and distinct; for since the black man's status in America was both assigned and final, the white man's mode was irrelevant to him. That is why much "black behavior" remains vestigially and cryptically survival-oriented.

Q: *We've used the term, "alternate lifestyles," but what you are saying is that each style is independent and legitimate in its own right.*

LINCOLN: Precisely. Whatever people learn to do in order to cope is legitimate. This is what culture is. Culture is simply the transmission, from one generation to another, of ways of coping with an environment, which may, incidentally, include other people who are either hostile or indifferent to your existence. If you happen to live in America, you probably use a four-pronged instrument called a fork; but if you happen to live in Formosa, you use an instrument called chopsticks. Who is to say that chopsticks are better than forks, or vice versa? To eat and survive is the crucial thing.

Q: *What can white, middle-class persons, those in the mainstream, learn from black culture?*

LINCOLN: It depends upon what they want to learn, or whether. White people have the opportunity to learn, first of all, that contemporary white, Western culture is not the only possible way of existence, that it is not the only authentic cul-

* Diaspora = those who are scattered to other areas.

ture. Our technology, for example, is quite advanced, while our systems of human relations are retarded. Our technology has reached the point of diminishing returns and threatens to destroy us all because we have no adequate consensus of values to regulate its use at the level of social and interpersonal relations. The cold, impersonal imperviousness which characterizes American technological "success" is not a feature of black culture.

But another word about cultural inventiveness and the art of survival. Take the matter of barbecue, which is something that most Southerners claim to know a great deal about, but very few know much about its origin. Barbecue originated in the efforts of the black slave to cope with an adverse reality. Being a slave and on a very limited diet, he soon learned that if he could "borrow" a pig and drag it off to the woods and roast it over a pit of coals, if there was no flame and the smoke was properly diffused, his cooking would go undetected, and with patience he could have a very succulent dish. The herbs that he found in the swamps and bayous added flavor to the meat drippings and became "barbecue sauce." The art was improved and perfected over the generations. So it came to be that the best barbecue in the country is made in the South and made by black people, whose long experience in survival technique produced a cultural invention which transcends all cultural bounds.

Q: *Are Blacks conditioned so that they have a special sensitivity to human relationships?*

LINCOLN: "Conditioned" is a laboratory word and probably ought not to be applied to black people. However, my admittedly subjective evaluation probably suggests that black people as a whole are more capable of a broader spectrum of emotions than white Americans. They seem to be more sensitive to human beings as "people" rather than as units or statistics; and they know about "human conditions" rather than abstract social or sociological theory. Although I have done no formal studies on the matter, I suspect that because Blacks have in the recent past suffered the conditions of slavery, they are more experienced in human misery and therefore are more sensitive to it. I say, "in the more recent past," because while practically all white cultures, too, have at one time or another undergone the slave experience, the black experience in formal slavery is much nearer the surface than that of most white Americans.

Q: *Let's talk about the relationship of this black consciousness to the black churches. Does this new consciousness, in this country anyway, stem in large part from the black churches?*

LINCOLN: Black consciousness does not necessarily begin in the church. As a matter of fact, the black church, like the white church, has been, for the most part, a very conservative institution. Because the church by its nature tends to conserve prevailing values, the black church has tended to fit the black experience into the existing requirements of the prevailing expression of the faith. Inevitably, this is where the black church ran into very grave difficulty, because the interpretation of the faith that the Blacks received from their white slave masters and others who benefited by their labor was inconsistent with a rendering of the faith not tainted with economic interests. Nevertheless, because Blacks were good Christians, and because they often accepted the white man's teaching that it was the God-ordained lot of black folks to suffer in this life, whenever the black church came under white sponsorship it remained essentially a docile, conservative institution.

There has been an abrupt change in the way the black church, as distinct from the Negro church, looks at reality The black church is now for the first time seriously engaged in the reconstruction of Christian theology. This is a very necessary enterprise, I think, because the whole thrust of theology in America has heretofore been written and preached as if black people did not exist. American theology has been a completely white-oriented interpretation of the faith. It has been completely oblivious of the religious dimensions of the white-over-black syndrome in Christian America. American theology has always been European-oriented. And we still tend to feel that no American theological scholar has really completed his training unless he has spent a year in Germany or Switzerland or elsewhere on the Continent. My point is that since theology represents a formal attempt to interpret the faith and say what it means, the meaning of the Christian faith that one finds in contemporary Germany or Switzerland or Edinburgh or Rome, for that matter, is not a meaning that is necessarily helpful to a black Christian in America in understanding or coming to terms with his existential situation. In consequence, American theology tends to be irrelevant to BlackAmericans. American theologians have spent thousands of pages and innumerable discourses in addressing themselves to the meaning of Buchenwald, for example, but they have never seriously addressed themselves to the question of 350 years of human slavery in this country, or to its dreadful aftermath.

It seems to me that American theology and the American church have striven for irrelevancy to the spiritual needs of black Christians, and for that reason the efforts of "bridging the gap" between black and white Christians tend to have a superficial ring. There is not a single major American theologian who has taken as his point of departure the slave experience which clouded the expression of the faith in this country for centuries, and which still compromises Christian relations to this day. Until American theology is willing to help American Christianity come to terms with so obviously an important experience in our common history, neither Whites nor Blacks will be optimally benefited by what American theology has to say.

Q: *Could a black religious theology have a different mode than the analytic, rational discourse that we're familiar with from white, European culture?*

LINCOLN: First, I don't think the style of theology is what is of critical importance. If you are suggesting that the last word, from the point of view of historicity, rational procedure, and logic has already been written and that there is no possibility of departure from this Holy Writ, I would certainly disagree.

In the first place, we keep rewriting what has already been written, and not necessarily with refinement. Each season brings its annual flood of "new" interpretations of "settled" issues that have nothing to do with the questions we want most to know about. Why then would it seem strange if black theologians, using the same tools, but coming from perspectives and experiences quite different from the white theologians, should arrive at different conclusions? For the first time in American history we now have a substantial school of well-trained black scholars writing theology. The black church has always had a theology to sustain it, of course, but it was a "preached" theology; it has not been what you would call "rational" or "systematic" for the obvious reason that these are categories of a sophisticated Western epistemological* mode scarcely evident in the culture at large, and certainly quite limited among slaves who were denied even the possession of Bibles lest they somehow teach themselves to read. But times

* Epistemology = the study of knowledge.

changed, and in the past ten years the output of black scholars has begun to give some indication of what America lost through her short-sighted policy of keeping all Blacks illiterate. Most intellectuals are concerned with some aspect of racial or ethnic identity and Christian meaning, and it was inevitable that some should turn their attention to the reconstruction of Christian theology; for if the faith is to endure as one faith, American theology must speak as effectively to Blacks in their condition as it does to Whites.

Q: Does theology, in your meaning, include ethics?

LINCOLN: Theology must include whatever it is that man can say about God on the basis of insight of divine disclosure. If God is a moral being, theology must have something to say about ethics. That is why the question of theodicy* is important. What is the meaning of black suffering? Why do the wicked seem to prosper? I am suggesting that traditional white theology has always interpreted the faith in a manner consistent with the prevailing white understanding of manifest destiny for the Christian West, and that this white theology made Christianity relevant to black people only in the most indirect and obscure kind of way. Only to the degree that a black man could be conceived as a kind of degraded white man could he be in any sense heir to God's promise in the new world a-building in the West. The ethical absurdity in all this is manifest in the point of view that Blacks as Blacks are not quite legitimate in themselves, but they may take on spiritual, social, economic, and political relevance through prescribed kinds of associations with Whites.

Q: Do you feel that the black middle class has been more imitative of the white middle class than it has been faithful to black ethnic identity?

LINCOLN: Of course. For the greater part of our history, black people in general, and the black middle class in particular, looked to the white middle class as a reference group for acceptable behavior and cultural style. There is nothing strange about this when one remembers that the black experience in America has been an experience in which there has been little opportunity to observe or to know about other possible ways of behaving. So strong was the white middle-class influence that even the poorest Blacks, for all their lack of status and power, joined the white middle class in looking down on the so-called poor white

* Theodicy = the study of the problem of evil.

trash and hating them for being poor and thus violating the image of what a "white man" ought to be. The black middle class could never be "White," but it knew by the most intimate observation how "white people" ought to act; and anyone, Black or White, who failed to measure up to the chimerical "white" ideal automatically forfeited the respect of the black middle class. Black middle-class values distinct from those of the white middle class are a recent phenomenon, indicative, I believe, of a growing sense of security Blacks are now realizing in accepting their blackness and finding value in being who they are rather than in hoping to be mistaken for who they are not.

Q: Are you saying that this makes it legitimate for the black middle class today to imitate whites?

LINCOLN: I am saying it is not a matter of legitimacy. In the future I see in America, Blacks and Whites are likely to imitate each other. The options are broader because today's Blacks have greater opportunity to participate meaningfully in culture-bearing activities, and the recognition of black achievement and innovation is not so severely stigmatized as before. We no longer need necessarily conceive of the white middle class as representing the *summum bonum** of human behavior. We are much better educated, much better traveled. We know a great deal more about ourselves as black people. In a free society such as this one can become, the black middle class has a perfect right to choose its own models; but it will inevitably contribute models as well. The evidence of this is already quite strong in some cross-cultural behaviors we take for granted.

Q: But did Blacks in this country not have a number of ethnic models? Michael Novak and others seem to be saying there was not just one white model but you had Germans, Russians, and others. Were those models not available to Blacks?

LINCOLN: As far as Blacks were concerned, the lines in this country were drawn, not among ethnic groups of European derivation, but between racial groups, that is to say, Blacks and Whites. So to the black man striving to be "American," whether in Birmingham or in Boston, whether the "ideal American" was of Irish descent, British, French, German, or whatever, the thing of critical importance was that he was White, and that *all* white men held peculiar advantages over *all* others who were not White.

* Summum bonum = the highest good.

You can test this by so recent a thing as our experiences in World War II. We were at war with the Germans, and the Germans were killing Americans all over the place. BlackAmericans were impressed into the American army for our common defense; but black soldiers guarding German prisoners here in the South could not even enter the restaurants where the "hated" German prisoners were fed. BlackAmerican soldiers were demeaned in the very presence of the enemy by being required to eat behind segregating curtains on troop trains, while the white German "enemy" enjoyed all available comforts and amenities. There wasn't a black man in this country during World War II and after who would have gotten half as much "consideration" as the most fanatic Nazi or as a "Communist" if he found himself on the wrong side of the tracks after dark. From the black perspective it has never made much difference whether you were ethnically German or Polish or Irish or what not; the difference was whether you were White or Black. Being Irish *and* Black, or English *and* Black, never quite made a difference, either, as tens of thousands of half-black ethnics can testify. For in the unforgiving eyes of a race-minded society they are all "Negroes."

Q: Do you think, then, that the fuss about ethnic groups being rejected or ignored points to a real problem?

LINCOLN: I will put it this way: whenever black protest becomes tiresome or begins really to disturb the American conscience, by coincidence or by strategy other "alienated" groups seem compelled to get into the act and siphon off attention to themselves and their oppressed condition. We have seen some interesting examples of this in the past decade. It used to be pretty well agreed that the BlackAmerican was at the very bottom of the heap in terms of economics, social status, public and private hostility, social justice—in fact, in just about everything. But when it began to appear that the nation was finally ready to do something substantial about racial oppression, we were suddenly confronted with the demands of a proliferation of other groups who found themselves even more niggerized and more in need of liberation than America's *traditional* niggers!

Q: Has the rise in consciousness of these ethnic groups , including Indians and Chicanos, depended on and risen out of black struggle?

LINCOLN: I do not intend to criticize the efforts on the part of other ethnic groups to better themselves, and my reference included some groups that are not ethnic. But certainly there are some groups seeking "liberation" whose liberty has never been seriously compromised. Certainly this would not include such obviously oppressed groups as Chicanos and Indians. As a matter of fact, it is statistically possible that for the first time in our history Blacks as a group are no longer totally at the bottom of the socioeconomic heap. But you must be aware of the well-established American tradition that all other ethnic groups ride on the shoulders of the Blacks at the bottom. They do not necessarily depend on Blacks or exploit Blacks in the effort to change circumstances for themselves, but because of the way this society is structured, any black mobility must push against whatever is in front of it or on top of it. Blacks are the available bedrock; so if the volcano heaves at the bottom and the Blacks move up a notch, then all the groups above them are moved up a notch. But their status relative to each other tends to remain the same. I think this is changing. More and more Blacks are managing to *trickle up and around* rather than pushing against the dead weight of tradition. They find new places in the social and economic interstices not yet available to the black group as a whole. It used to be said that the really good life in America was reserved for "Mighty few white folk and no niggers at all!" There are some signs that this ancient aphorism will one day need to be modified.

Q: Are you fairly optimistic, then, that black consciousness is being a big help to Blacks and will continue to be so?

LINCOLN: I think that black consciousness has been the BlackAmerican's greatest stride toward freedom in the last hundred years. It is of the greatest importance to understand that until black people began to value themselves, the hope and expectation that they would be valued by others was simply a small and plaintive voice crying in the American wilderness. Other ethnic groups were learning this by experience while Blacks were still hoping it wasn't so. When the Italian in "Little Italy" went out into the world to seek his fortune, and the people called him a "Wop" and made fun of his language and his clothes and the food he ate, back home in Little Italy was an ethnic community which valued him, which spoke his language, relished his kind of food, and thought his clothes becoming. So the so-called Wop was strengthened and given a sense of security by the love and appreciation of the ethnic group which claimed him.

This was true of the Chinese, the Greeks, and most other ethnic groups in this country save the Blacks. The reference group for black people was always white people, so when the black kid confronted the world beyond the ghetto and people out there made fun of his hair, and made fun of his clothes or his food or the fact that he didn't speak English like an Etonian, when he went back home the people *there* laughed at him, too! Because they had been so degraded by the racism inherent in American life they had no appreciation of themselves except insofar as they saw themselves as like Whites. The BlackAmerican could find no support for his peculiar identity anywhere until he learned to accept and live with his blackness and to find value in his own cultural perspectives. Lo-then-and-behold, if you please! At first this "cultural nationalism" was taken for

madness! (Who in his right mind could want to be black?) But when it became apparent that some Blacks really *believed* "Black is beautiful!" other ethnic groups began to borrow their style, a pretty clear indication of respect. Some Caucasians have even tried to grow Afros, and there have been other little cultural borrowings. For example, Blacks call a person who looks black but harbors white sentiments an "Oreo" (from the Oreo cookie, which is chocolate, or "black," on the outside, and cream-filled, or "white," on the inside). Now it has developed that a person who is Indian, or "red," in appearance, but who has "white" sentiments, is called an "apple." And finally, in New York so many white people are now eating "soul food" (euphemism for the once despised and ridiculed diet of the black poor) that in order to find soul food you have to go to the avant garde white restaurants—the people who eat at the black chicken shacks can't afford soul food any more. But then, being black always was expensive!

Suggestions For Digging Into The Issue

Discussion Questions

1. What is your reaction to the statement that the chief distinction in America has always been the one between black and white and not that between ethnic groups? Why are many whites oblivious to this distinction?

2. How do you react to the statement that attempts at dialogue, like those often organized between blacks and whites from different churches, are superficial? What could be done on a more serious level to enable blacks and whites to understand each other? If racism is the problem, what can be done to help the racists?

3. How do you feel about the statement: "Whatever people learn to do in order to cope is legitimate"? Does this view make even white mannerisms legitimate? How far can this view be carried? For instance, would it make legitimate such kinds of behavior as making "white lightning" in an illegal still, or working through the Mafia?

4. How would you answer the question: What can whites learn from blacks?

5. This interview might suggest that only culture and style matter, but what legal or social reforms need to be made to ensure greater freedom for blacks in this country?

Series on Black Theology

Ask the pastor or other staff members in your local congregation to help you plan a series of sessions on black theology. The sessions might be for the benefit of the entire congregation and not alone youth. Think about the possibilities of selecting a book on the subject that might be made available for persons to read as background material for the sessions. Almost every community will have black religious spokesmen who can act as resource leaders. Consider also the possibility of using films on this subject. The foregoing interview with Dr. Lincoln could also be considered background reading for participants. Some of the questions in the interview might also be put to blacks who are acting as speakers in a symposium or panel.

Black-White Consultation

Try to identify changes that can be made in your local community that would benefit minorities and make for better relations between blacks and whites and between the dominant group and subgroups. One way to approach this is to set up a joint consultation. Invite an equal number of blacks and whites, or whites and members of minority groups, to a session where these problems could be discussed. Ask one black and one white (youth, presumably) to sit together to talk about what the problems are, dividing the groups into pairs. After twenty or thirty minutes, assemble the entire group and try to list some of the problems identified. Then begin to plan for action proposals that would lead to changes in these areas.

Black History Discussion

Plan one or more sessions on black history, or U.S. history from a black perspective. Such discussions could be heplful whether your group is black, white, or integrated. Check the extra resources that follow for materials to use. The *Black Chronicle*, for example, could show how particular events might have a different meaning from the black and white perspectives. This discussion could be related to what is happening now in the world, nation, or your community to understand why different groups or subgroups interpret events differently, how the media can responsibly interpret events to the satisfaction of the total public, and how the church can help to bridge the communication gap.

Additional Resources

Books listed (many are in paperback) are generally available from bookstores and/or local public libraries. Rental and/or sale prices of other Additional Resource items are available from distributors; their addresses are listed at the back of the book.

Feature Films

Nothing but a Man (b/w, 92 min. Audio/Brandon). Personal struggle of southern black and his wife in society hostile to them.

Black Girl (color, 107 min. Cinema 5). Drama of a black American family.

Sounder (color, 100 min. Fox). Story of survival of a southern black family, sharecroppers, during the Depression era.

Short Films

From the Inside Out (b/w, 24 min. McGraw-Hill). Black teenagers comment as camera ranges over their community.

To Be Black (b/w, 54 min. McGraw-Hill). ABC-TV documentary reveals resentments and frustrations of black Americans.

Still a Brother: Inside the Negro Middle Class (b/w, 90 min. McGraw-Hill). A black crew made this film depicting life and problems of the black middle class.

Black History: Lost, Stolen, or Strayed? (color, 54 min. BFA). Bill Cosby discusses contributions of blacks that are not in history books.

Now Is the Time (b/w, 36 min. UCC Office for Audio-Visuals; also Mass Media). History and struggle for black first-class citizenship.

Black World (color, 53 min. BFA). In interviews with Mike Wallace of CBS News, black man's position in world is examined.

What Do You People Want? (color, 30 min. Impact). Black liberation movement's (Black Panther Party) angry indictment of white oppression.

"I Have a Dream": The Life of Martin Luther King (b/w, 30 min. BFA). CBS-TV portrayal of this dedicated man and the forces that brought him to leadership of his people.

The Growth of Political Awareness: Malcolm X (color, 23 min. Association Films). CBS presentation on the tenets of Malcolm X.

Black Boy (b/w, 30 min. BFC-TV Films). Ossie Davis reads from Richard Wright's classic.

Filmstrips

Interpretations: The Me Nobody Knows (color, Teaching Resources).

New Goals for Black Americans (color, Current Affairs Films).

Slides

Contemporary Black Painters and Sculptors (20 slides, Educational Dimensions).

Tapes

Dick Gregory: An Interview by Three Black Reporters (33 min. Pacifica #589).

The Role of the Black American Woman in America (50 min. Pacifica #ALW750).

California Black Leadership Conference: The Role of the Church in the Black Revolution (58 min. Pacifica #AP1181).

Black Power and White Trickery (52 min. Pacifica #591).

I Have a Dream—Martin Luther King (17 min. Pacifica #AS1166).

The Changing Black Citizen (53 min. Center for Cassette Studies).

Black Militant Ideologists (27 min. Center for Cassette Studies).

Transparencies

Great American Negroes (set of six, Society for Visual Education).

Afro-American History, Part 2 (set of ten, AEVAC).

Study Prints

Contemporary Art by Afro-Americans (10 prints, The United Presbyterian Church in the U.S.A.).

Records

Black Man in America: An Interview with James Baldwin (Miller-Brody #QCREDO).

The Black Experience (6 records, Miller-Brody #T3002).

Black Pioneers in American History, Vols. 1 & 2 (Caedmon #TC1252 and #TC1299).

Lorraine Hansberry on Her Art and the Black Experience (Caedmon #TC1352).

The Poetry of Langston Hughes (Caedmon #TC1272).

Games

Blacks and Whites (3–4 players, Dynamic Design). "Monopoly"-type board game using real estate as base of power.

The Black Experience (2–4 players, Theme Productions). American black history is basis of this board-type game.

Simulation

Encountertapes for Black/White Groups (five 1½-hr. sessions, 8–10 persons, Human Development Institute). Going beyond racial games to real meeting.

Charts

Picto-History of Black Americans (4 parts, color, Civic Education Service).

A Gallery of Great Afro-Americans (50 parts, color, Pitman Publishing Corp.).

Multimedia Kit

Black Americans in Government (5 filmstrips, 5 records, 5 portraits, teacher's manual, McGraw-Hill).

Drama

Proud Heritage on Parade by Kathlyn Gay (Contemporary Drama). Pageant about black history.

Books

The Black Poets (New York: Bantam).

The Black Man in America (Glenview, Ill.: Scott, Foresman).

Afro-American History, Past to Present (New York: Scribners).

Young and Black in America ed. Rae P. Alexander (New York: Random House).

Contemporary Black Artists in America by Robert Doty (New York: Dodd, Mead).

Black Drama in America: An Anthology ed. Darwin Turner (New York: Fawcett World).

The Black Revolt: The Civil Rights Movement, Ghetto Uprisings, and Separatism by James A. Geschwender (Englewood Cliffs, N.J.: Prentice-Hall).

Quest for a Black Theology (Philadelphia: United Church Press, Pilgrim Press).

Autobiography of Malcolm X tr. by Alex Haley (New York: Grove Press). Also available in a Grove Press edition prepared for grades 9 up edited by Alex Haley.

Dick Gregory's Political Primer by Dick Gregory, ed. James McGraw (New York: Harper & Row).

No More Lies: The Myth and the Reality of American History by Dick Gregory, ed. James McGraw (New York: Harper & Row).

Newspaper Packet

Black Chronicle. A packet of 14 newspapers, in a "you are there" format, reporting important events in black history as if reported on the day they happened. Newspaper packet, $2.50; study guide, $1, available from: Division of Publication, United Church of Christ, 1505 Race Street, Philadelphia, Pa. 19102).

Masculinity and Racism—
Breaking Out of the Illusion

BY DANIEL H. KRICHBAUM

Only a few years ago, the values and lifestyle of the white middle-class male were considered the epitome of American culture. Today they are being challenged, indeed attacked—and paradoxically, by the very groups that once admired them or took them as a model. Blacks, women, students, minorities of various kinds now see middle-class white men as the source of one of the nation's overriding domestic problems—the problem, namely, of racism.

I

Those who protest against this accusation have simply failed to trace the problem to its roots. Sociological and psychological studies have made it abundantly clear that racism, in both its individual and its institutional forms, does in fact originate in the values and lifestyle of white middle-class America. For racism goes deep. As one student of our society puts it, "Far from being the simple delusion of a bigoted and ignorant minority, racism is a set of beliefs whose structure arises from the deepest levels of our lives—from the fabric of assumptions we make about the world, ourselves, and others" (Joel Kovel: *White Racism: A Psycho-History* [Pantheon, 1970], p. 3). In other words, racism exists *when one group views its cultural values, lifestyles, and socio-economic self-interests as superior to those of other groups and then (overtly or covertly) implements these assumptions through societal norms and institutions.*

The racism evident in our white-dominated economic, political and religious institutions must certainly be dealt with. But here I am concerned mainly with cultural racism—that emerging from the values on which the white, middle-class American male identity role is based. Attempts to end institutional racism will be of little avail unless the attitudes and actions that stem from misplaced values and confused standards are eliminated.

Let me illustrate the nature of cultural racism by analyzing just one of the values of middle-class white America: the enormous importance it places on male employment. From early childhood, white males are taught that in his own eyes and in society's a man's worth depends largely on his having a job. Male children of all ages are pushed to do well in school, not in order to learn more about the world but in order to acquire "a good job" when they graduate. "Are you going to grow up and be a doctor like your dad"—or a judge or a business manager? But if a person has been brought up to believe that a man must have a job to be worthwhile, he will consider those who are unemployed inferior. Thus, whether their plight is ascribed to laziness, lack of training, or educational deprivation, unemployed blacks are obviously not as masculine as employed whites. Like the crippled, the blind, or the mentally handicapped, they are deficient in their capacity to be fully male.

Here is a vicious circle. Whites who believe that jobs define worth unconsciously apply this standard to others, to the poor or black community as a whole. Blacks are trapped. Not only are many of them unemployed; they are less employable because they cannot prove their worth without a job. Ultimately, it matters little whether or not whites consciously believe that blacks are equal. White males in industrial decision-making positions may say that "color makes no difference," but if they believe deeply that the job makes the man, they will contribute to racist policies. For they will be reluctant to hire those without good employment records (i.e., black people), will be disinclined to recruit in the black community, and will hesitate to establish apprentice programs.

II

The white middle-class idea that job defines worth is connected with other values. Aggressiveness, competitiveness, acquisition of power, and a sense of responsibility—these are the norms for the white male. They are thought of as positive characteristics; but let us look at their disadvantages. Generally speaking, men consider themselves responsible if they "provide for" their families. This role of provider has developed over the centuries, and men are now socialized to accept it. But responsibility is linked almost totally with the family's material welfare—rarely with meeting the emotional needs of family members. Moreover, "responsibility" entails decision-making; if he is a "man," *he* will make the decisions. It follows that, while the male's responsibility for others may be positive, women and children are kept within rather stringent boundaries.

In return for his "responsible" behavior, a middle-class man is accorded many favors by society. Usually he does not have to worry about the "trivial" aspects of life, since his wife takes care of the house and the children; so he is free to pursue a career and gain status. When he comes home from work, he expects to indulge in pleasurable hobbies, such as golf or gardening. Of course there are times when the washing machine needs to be fixed or the kids have to be brought into line. But generally the family shows him respect. He is to be left alone to read the paper, and the children are to keep quiet. These favors and privileges are costly to the man who receives them. First, he must earn the living his family accepts as its right; whether he finds his work fulfilling is not a primary question. Second, he may have very little time for his family or his hobbies. His job may so drain his physical and psychic energies that he cannot contribute positively to familial relationships.

More, the "work syndrome" dehumanizes the man himself. His work defines his existence. He never really discovers who he, as a unique individual, is. It is absurd to think that a man "lives" a good life because he can devote almost all his hours to his job while his wife looks after family concerns. Too often he does not even have time to enjoy the material possessions he is able to acquire. In short, the middle-class white male is prostituted through a socialization process which falsely labels his existence masculine and worthwhile.

Competitiveness is another norm of "maleness." Here the assumption is that the less competitive male is weak and unmanly, therefore must be content with leftovers from the pool of limited material resources. The reward of successful competitive endeavor is power—power to make decisions not only for oneself but for others too. To be powerful shows that one is strong.

The white middle-class concept of manhood also implies aggressiveness. A man should not be passive—should not sit idly by and let events shape him. He is always to be the initiator (particularly, of course, in male-female and adult-child relationships). Being aggressive, he will also be independent; that is, he will remain calm and unemotional in work situations. But this requirement of emotionless detachment is likely to be disastrous for the man concerned. Ingrained to the exclusion of other emotions, such detachment tends to stunt his personality. And more often than not, it leads him to conform to the status quo in his climb up the success ladder.

How does all this affect the integrity of what a man does? Is the white middle-class man's production productive? He is taught to consider himself useless and his life meaningless unless his production fills a need for others. But today multitudes of men are small cogs in an industrial machine that produces what no one needs; and inducing people to produce or consume things that do not meet human needs destroys the integrity of both producer and consumer.

III

Such, then, are the white middle-class masculine values and lifestyle. Let me now try to show more clearly how they contribute to racism. The predicament facing whites today is that actions by individuals which are not directly antiracist serve to foster racism. There is no in-between: an act is either antiracist or racist. To do nothing is to give the racist ball another push.

The first link between racism and white middle-class norms is the ease with which white males dismiss both urgent societal issues and the unsatisfactoriness of their own lives. Meeting the "material-status needs" of their families takes all the time and energy they have to give. So long as men understand their responsibility as including the raising of their status and income to the maximum, they will be unable to combat racism, because doing so takes time for evaluation, energy for commitment, and courage for engagement.

Again, the white male tends to view responsibility as resting only on his shoulders, and he glories in meeting it successfully. But because the material and familial requirements on him are so great, he is not about to help anyone else. "That's his problem. I've got my own worries. If he can't handle his responsibility, too bad." Remarks like this imply that the speaker is important, that he acknowledges no moral responsibility for others, and that he looks upon anyone who fails in responsibility as inferior. Thus anyone who falls short of the white middle-class norm of maximum familial responsibility is lazy, immature, maladjusted—inferior; that is, poor people are inferior and most blacks are inferior. Clearly, many white rationalizations for racism grow out of this unexamined and misplaced value.

Consider, next, the norm of competitiveness. Competition is not necessarily dehumanizing, but the white masculine competitive style is, because worth and status are measured by its results. Consequently, no intrinsic value attaches to human relationships, for these become part of the competitive struggle for survival. People are used and manipulated; they are of little worth unless they provide an edge against the competition. When one's colleagues are pawns and one's neighbors the competition, those removed from the struggle have little value. The concerns of the poor and/or the blacks are of no concern unless these groups either get in the way or can be used. In any case, since competition is a norm for white males, minorities can be exploited in order to win. After all —so the rationalizations go—men are competitive by nature, and responsibility for self and family depends on successful competition.

This dehumanizing competitiveness often gives rise—though subtly and unintentionally—to racist decisions on the part of institutions. In business, for example, decisions are based only on the profit margin; in the fields of community service and governmental organizations, only on institutional expansion and perpetuation. Thus racism is reinforced.

White middle-class values have results in the area of relationships also. On the one hand, power exists at every level of human enterprise, and the rules governing its use are of critical importance. In our society, it becomes the means of fulfilling the white man's distorted self-image. On the other hand, he refuses to use his power for the benefit of others when such use seems to threaten his own security. This is a curious paradox in that it perpetuates institutional racism—if not through direct exploitation, then through a hands-off, scapegoating stance that condones exploitation of others.

This ambivalence over power has several side effects. Fear of failure or conflict, fear of betraying his feelings of insecurity and weakness to the world prompt the middle-class white male to refrain from emotional expression. Indeed, he accepts repression of emotion as normal and therefore looks down on people (such as blacks and Latinos) who tend to vent their feelings freely.

Finally, because they are dissatisfied with their way of life, middle-class white males are angry. The suggestion that their lifestyle is wanting puts them on the defensive. Even so, they are being increasingly pressured to reevaluate their values. It is time that they considered alternative patterns of behavior. Where can these be found?

IV

A new *image* of white masculinity—based perhaps on a biblical or historical character, or on some speculative vision of the "ideal" male—will not do, for images themselves enslave when they are taken too seriously. Indeed, the fact that the present code of male behavior has been turned into an image—has become *the* model to be uncritically accepted—is part of our society's racist problem.

Let me therefore limit myself to offering not rules but behavioral suggestions. It seems to me that presenting the white middle-class male with a choice of lifestyles will best advance his liberation *from* false standards and *for* the benefit of society.

First, then, I suggest that the white male *develop group consciousness*. The average person is unable to struggle alone—at least successfully; he needs the support of his fellow human beings, whether by way of encouragement or of confrontation with different ways of living. Group consciousness counters distorted notions of individuality; it implies that the goal of life is meaningful human interaction. Because it encourages a sense of community, it frees group members from the burden of believing that they are required to meet all the needs of others.

Second, I suggest that we *reduce our expectations on the material level*. As I said above, male identity in our society is based primarily not on vocation itself but on the rewards of vocation; manliness is equated with possessions and status. But the liberated male will not look to how much he can earn but to how little time and energy he needs to expend in order to attain an adequate standard of living. Defining and maintaining a *minimal standard of living* frees men to develop their personal interests, to help solve community problems, and to care actively for others. The fact is, jobs and material resources are no longer plentiful in America. Overvaluing them creates insecurity, mindless competition, and physical and emotional illness. But our society still has areas of plenty; interpersonal relationships, social action, and emotional and intellectual satisfactions are available to all comers.

Third, I suggest what has been called the "*creative expression of personhood*." This means that we can discard the unproductive and functionless images of rationality, coolness under pressure, angry conformity—all the other inhibiting restrictions that warp us. After all, there is no logical reason why men should not express various emotions in various ways. The "creative expression of personhood" also means honesty about productive life in that it distinguishes productivity from employment. The liberated male will define as *productive* only that part of his time, energy, and skill that he devotes to meeting the needs caused by injustice, disease, and social callousness.

Fourth, I suggest *coping with community problems.* Until they undertake to help solve the crucial problems of their local communities, middle-class American males will remain the slaves of a false image. Today, the white community is made up of a ruling elite and an apathetic majority. Both maintain and foster racism—the one by its decisions, the other by its scapegoating and its unthinking implementation of those decisions. Nowadays, the average white middle-class male's

longing for self-determination is frustrated. He needs to redirect his frustration so as to end the elite's control over his community. It is through passionate involvement in community affairs that he will be able to liberate himself and his fellow Americans.

These suggestions of mine are made in the context of a pluralistic framework. No doubt some will be accepted, some rejected. But all of them have a common point of reference; namely, the white man's oppression of blacks, women, and youth. Recognition of his racism will be painful for the white, but it is both a crucial step toward the liberation of other men and a positive response to the powerful liberating movements in other segments of our society.

The Rev. Daniel H. Krichbaum is a pastor at Central United Methodist Church, Detroit. His article appeared originally in *The Christian Century,* January 10, 1973, and is reprinted here by permission.

Suggestions For Digging Into The Issue

Discussion Questions

1. Do you agree with the author's point of view that racism is embedded in the white masculine image and behavior? Why or why not?

2. Should we give up the values of aggressiveness, competitiveness, acquisition of power, and a sense of responsibility? Or should we simply balance these off with passivity, cooperation, appreciation of human relationships, and other values?

3. In what sense is it true that teenagers and students are also measured by productivity and therefore found wanting?

4. Does the writer here imply that blacks cannot compete or produce or gain and wield power? Does he attribute more influence to the white masculine person than he is really due?

5. What would be the result for middle-class family styles of living if the author's suggestions were followed for changing the white masculine image?

Debate

Ask a traditional defender of male American values (competitiveness and aggressiveness, for example) to debate someone arguing that these values need to be changed and modified. Another approach would be a three-way discussion, with a woman entering into the argument.

Role Play

Role play a family scene where the traditional image of the white male is played by the father. The situation might be any involving the making of a decision. After letting the role players express themselves as father, mother, and children, turn the situation around and have the father express the new image suggested at the end of the article. Afterward, let the group discuss the question whether given individuals, especially those who have reached middle age, are flexible enough to change their attitudes and behavior.

Biblical Discussion

Consider building one or more sessions around the implications of this article for Christian life. One way to approach such issues is to think of biblical characters and whether their actions reflected the "bad" white masculine image criticized by the writer of the article; then imagine how their behavior might have been different if they had been cooperative, passive, and so forth. Or discuss the figure of Jesus: which image does he come closest to?

Additional Resources

Books listed (many are in paperback) are generally available from bookstores and/or local public libraries. Rental and/or sale price of other Additional Resource items are available from distributors; their addresses are listed at the back of the book.

Feature Film

Man in the Gray Flannel Suit (color, 152 min. Films Inc.) Portrait of white-collar worker on Madison Ave. trying to get ahead.

Short Films

Friendly Game (b/w, 10 min. Mass Media). Interpretation of racist and capitalistic psychology embodied in chess game.

The Detached Americans (b/w, 33 min. UCC Office for Audio-Visuals; also Mass Media). Examines problem of apathy among middle-class Americans.

Mr. Grey (color, 10 min. Mass Media). White-collar worker comes to see himself as a convict.

If There Weren't Any Blacks You'd Have to Invent Them (b/w, 58 min. Mass Media). Morality play, set in cemetery, of young man entering society.

Tapes

Racism in Perspective (65 min. Pacifica #102).

Father James Groppi of Milwaukee Speaks (75 min. Pacifica #099).

The Emotional Roots of Racism (65 min. Pacifica #100).

Racism, Poverty, and Urban Collapse (50 min. Center for Cassette Studies).

Games

Ghetto (7–10 players, 2–4 hrs. Western Publishing).

Sunshine (20–35 players, 16–22 hrs. Interact).

Drama

I Am Waiting for a New World by Paul Nolan (Contemporary Drama). Fantasy about racism, social standing, and chance.

Books

Am I a Racist? by Fortuse Monte (New York: Association Press).

The Language of White Racism (Evanston, Ill.: McDougal, Littel & Co.).

Racism: A Casebook ed. F. R. Lapides (New York: Thomas Y. Crowell).

Beyond Racism by Whitney Young, Jr. (New York: McGraw-Hill).

White Racism: A Psycho-History by Joel Kovel (New York: Random House, Pantheon).

Racism: American Style (Philadelphia: United Presbyterian Church in the U.S.A.).

Institutional Racism in America ed. L. Knowles (Englewood Cliffs, N.J.: Prentice-Hall).

Los Hispanos: A Different Style

BY DANIEL ALVAREZ

They were told: "The Spanish are Catholic"; "The Spanish are always late"; "They are the mañana people." For many Americans *los hispanos* are known by these stereotypes. Vice versa, when I was living in Latin America I was told that almost all U.S. Americans were Protestant. Of course, those expressions don't represent reality. It is hard to believe that those kinds of misconceptions affect 15 million people in the United States. It is about time for the pepole of this country to discover who are *los hispanos.*

We understand that the Spanish-speaking population is sometimes confusing to the American public. We are frequently known as Mexicans, Mexican-Americans, Chicanos, Puerto Ricans, Cubans, etc. Although this variety of nationalities exists, a common ground of cultural patterns, language, and historic origin bring our nationalities together. Helping to reunite our groups is the fact of the social problems that we all confront. Facing the issues in urban America, many Spanish groups are beginning to work together toward the same goals. Let us examine some of the reasons and elements in the immigration and migration of the Spanish to and within America.

The Mexicans, the oldest Hispanic group, have a long history of participation in the working force in the United States. From the railroad tracks to the grape vineyards, thousands and millions have contributed to the economy. Their working conditions and the low salaries have been keeping them out of participation except as victims of a modern slavery. Many Mexicans move from the rural to the urban setting. Others come direct from Mexico trying to bypass the migrant stream. New generations of Mexican-Americans are beginning to enjoy some of the opportunities for education, jobs, etc. Some of them could be found even in suburbia. Still, the majority are very proud of their heritage, and many of them retain their Mexican citizenship.

The Puerto Ricans are coming without the immigration regulations of other nationalities. They are American citizens and have the right to move from the island of Puerto Rico to the mainland. Although this American citizenship is equal by law, thousands of Puerto Ricans are not enjoying the benefits of this nation. They are also proud of their Puerto Rican identity. They travel constantly between the island and the continent and keep afresh the elements of their culture and traditions.

Cubans are here mainly for political reasons. In the first part of the sixties a very high percentage were people with education or wealth. But in the second part a large number of the working class, fishermen, farm workers, etc., came too. They enjoy a different experience under the status of political refugees.

These three main groups have different hardships. For example, Mexicans have immigration problems. The U.S. requests them due to the need of manpower in this country and rejects them when this need is met. The Mexican-Americans with their identity problem often tend to feel like a different race (*La Raza*). Although legally citizens, Puerto Ricans find that their rights are limited according to the geographical area where they live. They look at the possibility of an ideal citizenship of their own, but at the same time face the realities of an island without the economic potential of self-support. Cubans have come out of a political struggle with the experience to participate in the political arena, but they lack the political rights and the feeling of belonging.

Other Latin-Americans: Colombians, Guatemalans, Chileans, Peruvians, etc., came looking for the American dream of education, money, success. Many of them found their dreams shattered by the present social struggle in our communities, but they are willing to pay the price, hoping that their children will have a better chance.

As I stated before, there is still a common ground for our people. The language unites our nationalities and makes us sing the same song. I found in situations of controversy between Anglos and *hispanos,* that when the latter changed to the Spanish language this created a real island of unity that allowed them to exercise their own interests. In a way, the language creates a peculiar characteristic similar to that which color gives to the blacks.

Another factor in our own style of life is the strong emphasis on family ties. Living in a society where the family structure is changing, the Hispanic family insists in preserving its own structure. The strong role of the man (sometimes distorted with the term *machismo*) is attractive to people from different styles of life. The woman is sensitive as a flower, but strong in her family role. The youngsters in the family await impatiently their time to be recognized as adults because the parental authority prolongs their attachment to the family structure.

These are *Los Hispanos:* a meaningful part in the industrial world of the United States. They are unrecognized politically and are socially ignored and neglected in the potential contribution of their talents. Themselves confused, they are persistent in their own culture and still trying to learn from another culture. Again, a silent and different community within the large community.

Suggestions For Digging Into The Issue

Discussion Questions

1. What is the stereotype of a Spanish-speaking American and how, as a Christian, ought one to react to such stereotypes?

2. Why do some Americans object to the use of a language other than English as un-American or somehow undesirable? Do you agree or disagree with these objections?

3. Would integration of *los hispanos* into the mainstream be a constructive social goal? Or do you think they should simply maintain a separate style of their own?

4. How do you feel about *los hispanos* who represent themselves as "La Raza" (a different race)?

Interview

Ask a Spanish-speaking person who is a member of the Spanish-speaking community (not just a teacher of Spanish, for example) to the group and interview him or her before the group. Ask about the distinctive style of *los hispanos* and what this style says about the people and their values. You may want to follow up with a visit to an an area of the community where *los hispanos* live, if there is one; or visit a church where Spanish is the preferred language.

Support Community Organizations

In many cities and parts of the country, community organizations work on issues affecting Spanish-speaking people in those communities. See if there are such organizations in your own part of the world; make contact and ask how you can be of help; and be prepared to join with them in providing services, solving problems, or resolving conflicts important to them.

Additional Resources

Books listed (many are in paperback) are generally available from bookstores and/or local public libraries. Rental and/or sale prices of other Additional Resource items are available from distributors; their addresses are listed at the back of the book.

Feature Film

Popi (color, 113 min. UA 16). Puerto Rican widower trying to raise two kids in ghetto.

Short Films

The World of Piri Thomas (color, 60 min. Indiana Univ.). Pleads for understanding of Puerto Rican ghetto life.

Children of the Revolution (b/w, 30 min. American Documentary Films). Cuban exiles and their lives and views.

Chicano (color, 27 min. McGraw-Hill). Four Chicanos proudly express how they feel.

Huelga! (color, 50 min. McGraw-Hill). Famous Delano Grape Strike.

Migrant (color, 52 min. NBC). Documentary of "rented slaves."

Mexican Americans: Quest for Equality (b/w, 29 min. Anti-Defamation League). Social and economic conditions.

Mexican Americans: An Historic Profile (b/w, 29 min. Anti-Defamation League). Traces history of Mexican Americans.

Rank and File (b/w, 15 min. Indiana Univ.). Fight for own labor union.

The Most Hated Man in New Mexico (color, 29 min. NBC). Former farm worker speaks for the Southwest poor.

Viva La Causa (color, 22 min. UCC Office for Audio-Visuals). Cesar Chavez and Joan Baez appear in this film on the United Farm Workers.

Filmstrips

Portrait of a Minority: Spanish Speaking Americans (2 parts, color, Scott Education).

Out of the Mainstream (6 parts, color, Warren Schloat).

Tapes

La Mula No Nacio Arisca (49 min. CSDI #255).

Who Is the Enemy? (40 min. CSDI #256).

The Cactus Curtain (45 min. CSDI #257).

Creative Non-Violence (20 min. CSDI #457).

The Educational Needs of the Chicanos (40 min. Pacifica #150).

The Distortion of Mexican-American History (37 min. Pacifica #101).

Pa'Lante: The Young Lords (32 min. Pacifica #WU0147.01).

Pa'Lanlante: Self-Determination for the Puerto Rican Colony in N.Y. (29 min. Pacifica #WU0147.03).

The Spanish Speaking Poor in an Urban Setting (15 min. Pacifica #021.5).

Cuba Must Go (30 min. National Center for Audio Tapes).

A Walk on the West Side (45 min. National Center for Audio Tapes).

Records

Cult Music of Cuba (Scholastic).

Songs and Dances of Puerto Rico (Scholastic).

Books

The Chicanos: Mexican American Voices ed. E. W. Ludwig (Baltimore: Penguin).

The Puerto Rican Poets (New York: Bantam).

The World of the Chicano ed. J. M. Cohen (Baltimore: Penguin).

New Comers by O. Handlin (Garden City, N.Y.: Doubleday).

Chicano by R. Vasquez (New York: Avon).

Writers on the New Cuba (Baltimore: Penguin).

Emergency Faces: The Mexican Americans by Y. A. Caluera (Dubuque, Iowa: William C. Brown Company).

Mexican American—An Awakening Minority by M. Servin (Beverly Hills, Calif.: Glencoe).

Palante! The Young Lords' Party (New York: McGraw-Hill).

Powwows and Peyote Help Indians Adjust to Life in the Big City

BY SUSAN MARGOLIES

Every morning before he leaves for work, Hubert Honane pauses on his doorstep to give thanks for the new day. The 55-year-old Hopi Indian offers corn—the Hopi symbol of birth—to the sun, the moon, and a deity known as the Spider Woman. "To us she acts as a guardian angel," Mr. Honane explains. His prayer completed, Mr. Honane can start his commute to the furniture-refinishing business he owns in Pasadena, California.

Although he has traded the open spaces of his native Arizona for the crowded, pollution-choked suburbs of Los Angeles, Mr. Honane has managed to transport to the city some of the customs that were so much a part of life on the reservation where he was born.

Indians have always had to struggle mightily to maintain their cultural identity in white America. Yet never has the task been so difficult as for the 350,000 Indians now living away from the reservation. Even though most have congregated in large cities seeking work, many urban Indians refuse to abandon traditional ways. Tribal customs, they say, can often smooth the transition to urban life by providing a link to the familiar and a way of fighting loneliness. "Indians on the reservation often take their traditions for granted, but here in the city they become essential for survival," says David Lester, a Creek who directs a Los Angeles group that relocates Indians to the city from the reservation.

Peyote Is Permitted

Unquestionably, it takes a heavy dose of determination to keep up tribal rituals in the city. Ernest Murdock, a 61-year-old Kickapoo living in Los Angeles, sometimes travels 200 miles to attend services at a Native American Church, a denomination that combines Indian and Christian beliefs. Church ceremonies often involve the use of peyote, a hallucinogenic agent derived from cactus plants. (Several states, including California, have ruled the drug's use as a religious sacrament is legal.)

Like many Indians, Mr. Murdock believes peyote has healing properties. When a member of his family is ailing and can't travel to the remote church, Mr. Murdock sometimes holds his own peyote ceremony. He brews peyote tea and shakes a sacred gourd to the rhythm of tape-recorded tribal songs. With the help of the sacramental tea, he says, the illness passes quickly. Although his citified version of the ceremony is a far cry from the real thing, he says that "when our ancestors went out on hunts they couldn't drag the whole reservation with them, so they had to improvise. That's what I do here in the city."

Another urban Indian who is learning to adapt is John Eagleshield, a 25-year-old Sioux born in South Dakota. When the walls of his New York City high-rise apartment begin to close in on him, Mr. Eagleshield takes off for the woods of New Jersey. There, a friend lets him use property on the banks of the Delaware River to build a "sweat lodge," or hut fashioned from rocks, branches, and a sacred blanket. The saunalike action of a fire inside the hut helps purify his soul along with his body, Mr. Eagleshield believes. He calls the ritual "an extensive prayer."

On more festive occasions, Mr. Eagleshield and his wife, Toni Lone Hawk, join up with dozens of Apache, Iroquois, Navaho, and Mohawk for a monthly powwow at a Manhattan branch of the YMCA. "Powwows for us are comparable to the white man's evening out at the Waldorf," says Mr. Eagleshield, who is a celebrated war dancer. The gatherings are sponsored by a group of Indian dancers and sometimes draw more than 200 non-Indian spectators.

Although his ancestors used the powwow dances to fire themselves up before a battle, Mr. Eagleshield finds them a good way of relaxing. Decked out in eagle feathers, he and the other dancers whirl and jump around the room to the beat of tom-toms and recorded songs. (To get his prized feathers, Mr. Eagleshield had to wait until he found a dead eagle on the reservation because federal law prohibits killing the birds.)

Bell Bottoms and Feathers

The dances are authentic, but some of the powwow rituals have been updated. The traditional honoring song, a centuries-old tribute to dead warriors, is now sung in memory of those who died in Vietnam. And many of the younger Indians prefer bell-bottom trousers and penny loafers to feathers and moccasins.

For some urban Indians, a powwow offers relief from the isolation they feel in the city. "It's often the only opportunity we get to keep bona fide contact with the reservation," says Wilbur Shongo, an elderly member of the Seneca tribe in upstate New York who attends the powwows regularly. Mr. Shongo, a Manhattan resident who has drifted from job to job over the years, says, "The only roots I really have are on the reservation."

But some city Indians contend tribal ceremonies should remain on the reservation. Ron Purley, director of the Indian Cultural Center at UCLA and a member of the Laguna tribe, returns to the New Mexico reservation where he was born at least four times a year for particularly sacred rituals. And, when a new officer is elected to the tribal council, Mr. Purley goes back to formally ask his permission to leave the reservation. In this way, he says, he shows his respect for tribal elders.

Sometimes, however, the reservation comes to the city. Leonard Crow Dog, a medicine man and a leader at the recent Wounded Knee confrontation, periodically visits various cities to make housecalls on his friends. He has a sliding fee scale that can be as little as a sack of flour, if that's all a patient can afford. The Indians regard him as a medium who can intercede with the spirits of their ancestors. His ministrations, they say, can reunite an estranged couple, locate lost objects, and restore health.

Mrs. Eagleshield recently consulted the medicine man after developing a stomach ailment. To prepare for the ceremony, the Eagleshields cleared their apartment of possessions in order to strike the proper note of humility. After stashing their furniture on the terrace, they brought in flowerpots filled with soil from Central Park to signify their ties with nature.

According to Sioux belief, the medicine man's diagnoses and treatments are dictated by an unseen spirit conjured up during the ceremony. At the Eagleshields' ceremony, Leonard Crow Dog was placed at the foot of a handmade altar with his hands and feet bound and a blanket draped over his head. After receiving spiritual advice, he cured Mrs. Eagleshield's stomach disorder by reciting a chant and administering herbs, she says.

"We Never Knock"

However, the Indian cultural heritage consists of more than elaborate ceremonies and brightly colored regalia. Informal tribal behavior habits also carry over to urban life. David Lester says that when he and his wife visit other Indians in the city, they simply drop in without calling in advance. "When we get there we never knock," he says. When something nice or lucky happens to a member of the family, the Lesters hold a "give away." According to custom, the happy person bestows gifts of cloth, blankets, and beadwork on friends and relatives "so that they may share in his joy," Mr. Lester says.

Moreover, Indian family ties—even in the city—are stronger than in white society. Among many tribes, cousins are viewed as brothers and sisters, and uncles are given the same right to discipline a child as the child's father has. And when Mr. Murdock's brother died, the Kickapoos held a ceremony in which Mr. Murdock was allowed to "adopt" another member of the tribe as his brother.

While pleasant traditions can help bridge the gap between the reservation and the city, they can't obliterate the prejudice many Indians encounter off the reservation. Some find the adjustment too difficult and return to their own people. To help dispel some of the old stereotypes and prejudices among whites and to awaken ethnic consciousness among Indians, the Eagleshields show films and lecture to both groups. Mrs. Eagleshield, who complains she is tired of having whites stare at her husband's braids, says, "Many people in this country still consider us blood savages." Once, at Mount Rushmore the couple were eating lunch and a woman ran over to Mr. Eagleshield and squeezed his arm. "She just wanted to touch a real live Indian," she says.

This article appeared originally in *The Wall Street Journal*, June 5, 1973, and is reprinted here by permission. Susan Margolies is a staff reporter for that newspaper.

Suggestions For Digging Into The Issue

Discussion Questions

1. In what ways do these illustrations of contemporary Indian life differ from the usual stereotypes of Indians?

2. What do these descriptions say about an Indian style of life? Or are there many such styles?

3. What do these Indian styles have in common with styles growing out of the counterculture?

4. What could those with other lifestyles learn from contemporary Indians?

5. What stance should Christians take toward Indians, especially those who wish to retain their native religion? What does the term "Native American" imply about Indian identity?

Resource Persons

Check to see if there are offices of the Bureau of Indian Affairs (BIA) or of Volunteers in Service to America (VISTA) in your area. Professionals in these offices may be able to share information with you about Indians and their style of life. Obviously, the best source lies with Indians themselves. Many metropolitan areas have colonies of Indians, and usually reservations are well known in rural areas. Another source might be national or regional offices of home mission boards of major denominations.

Research

Assign different individuals the task of doing research on various aspects of Indian life, particularly contemporary Indians. The effort might result in one or more sessions on the contributions of Indians to our culture and to our religious understanding. The visual aspects could be exploited, too: posters, displays, and photos could be used to support discussion.

Field Trip

If there is an Indian reservation or community in your area, it might be worthwhile to make a visit there, with the goal of simply getting to know the people and seeing firsthand how they live and what their problems are. A contact in preparation for the visit is essential.

Another idea is to make a long trip out of a visit to a tribe or other Indian community. Since many youth groups schedule an annual bus trip to other parts of the country, you might put this on your agenda as a way of trying to learn from the Indian way of life (certainly any thought of evangelizing Indians should be put aside unless there are special conditions that make an evangelical visit appropriate). Careful preparation is needed for such a visit. Inquire at the office of the reservation about their policies on visits from the outside, permission requirements, and information that would prepare your group.

Additional Resources

Books listed (many are in paperback) are generally available from bookstores and/or local public libraries. Rental and/or sale prices of other Additional Resource items are available from distributors; their addresses are listed at the back of the book.

Feature Films

When the Legends Die (color, 107 min. Fox). Dramatic context for contrasting two distinctively American ways of life: white middle class and American Indian.

Tell Them Willie Boy Is Here (color, 111 min. Universal). A Paiute Indian on California reservation caught between tribal tradition and white man's law.

Hombre (color, 111 min. Films Inc.). Character study of white man raised among Apaches then forced back into white man's world.

Short Films

The Exiles (b/w, 72 min. McGraw-Hill). American Indians who have left their reservations and are caught between two cultures.

The North American Indian—Parts 1, 2, 3 (color, each part approx. 18–25 min. McGraw-Hill). A historical documentation of the treatment of the American Indian by the white man.

Geronimo Jones (color, 21 min. Learning Corp, of America). Young Indian caught between two worlds when he trades treasured Apache medallion for used television set.

Home of the Brave (color, 3 min. Pyramid). The 500-year story of a people is capsulized in this short film.

The Forgotten American (color, 25 min. UCC Office for Audio-Visuals; also Mass Media). Plight of the American Indian—lack of food, economic opportunity, health and education services—documented in this candid report.

The Long Trail (b/w, 30 min. BFC-TV Films). Sam Running Foot in his struggle to adjust to a society that neither understands nor wants him.

Transparencies

Indian Tribes and Cultures (Modern School Supply).
American Indian (set of 18, AEVAC).

Tapes

Disinherited and Dispossessed (59 min. Pacifica #BC0803).

Rolling Thunder Speaks (71 min. Pacifica #KU0022).

Chief Red Fox Remembers (64 min. Pacifica #BC0092).

The Singing Wire: American Indian Music Today (55 min. Pacifica #XX0050).

Indians on Alcatraz: The First Anniversary (36 min. Pacifica #AP1411).

The Indians: An Overview (60 min. Pacifica #AP1359).

Fragment from a Life in Poverty (23 min. Pacifica #AS1319).

American Indians and American History (51 min. Pacifica #A2151).

Indian Environmental Conference (44 min. Pacifica #BC0191).

Records

Red Hawk's Account of Custer's Last Battle (Caedmon #TC1365). Read by full-blooded Cherokee.

The Pueblo Indians (Caedmon #TC1327). A Pueblo chief tells legends and reads stories from tribal heritage.

Navajo Bird Tales as Told by Hosteen Clah Clee (Caedmon #TC1375). Folk tales as told by medicine man.

Little Wheel Spin and Spin (Vanguard #VSD79211). Buffy Sainte Marie, a Cree Indian, sings folk songs including "My Country 'Tis of Thy People You're Dying"—her statement in song about Indian affairs.

It's My Way (Vanguard #VSD79142). Includes "Now That the Buffalo's Gone," Buffy Sainte Marie's lament in song for past treatment of her people.

Chart

First American (Scholastic).

Map

Indian Americans (United Methodist Board of Missions).

Kit

Indian Art (EMI).

Books

The Search for an American Indian Identity: Modern Pan-Indian Movements by H. W. Hertzberg (Syracuse, N.Y.: Syracuse Univ. Press).

Disinherited: The Lost Birthright of the American Indian by Dale Van Every (New York: William Morrow).

The Magic World: American Indian Poems and Songs ed. Wm. Brandon (New York: William Morrow).

My Life as an Indian by J. Schultz (New York: Fawcett World).

Readings in the History of the American Indian (New York: Mss Information Corp.).

Indian—And Proud of It (New York: Lead Industries Assn.).

The Art of the Southwest Indians by Shuley Glubok (New York: Macmillan).

Custer Died for Your Sins by Vine Deloria, Jr. (New York: Avon).

We Talk, You Listen by Vine Deloria, Jr. (New York: Dell).

Bury My Heart at Wounded Knee: An Indian History of the American West by Dee Brown (New York: Bantam).

Periodical

Youth. The November 1973 issue is entirely devoted to Indian concerns. Single copies are available from United Presbyterian Church in the U.S.A., Witherspoon Building, Philadelphia, Pa. 19107.

The Young Worker—
Challenging the Work Ethic?

More than any other group, it appears that young people have taken the lead in demanding better working conditions. Out of a workforce of more than 85 million, 22½ million are under the age of 30. As noted earlier, these young workers are more affluent and better educated than their parents were at their age. Factually, that is nearly all that can be generalized about this group. But it is asserted by such authors as Kenneth Keniston, Theodore Roszak, Charles Reich, and others, that great numbers of young people in this age group are members of a counterculture. The President's Commission on Campus Unrest wrote that this subculture "found its identity in a rejection of the work ethic, materialism, and conventional social norms and pieties." Many writers have stressed the alleged revolt against work, "a new 'antiwork ethic' . . . a new, deep-seated rejection by the young of the traditional American faith in hard work." But empirical findings do not always support the impressionistic commentaries.

It is commonly agreed that there is a difference between the in-mode behavior of youth and their real attitudes. Many young people do wear beads, listen to rock music, and occasionally smoke pot, but few actually live in communes (and these few may be working very hard), and even fewer are so alienated that they are unwilling to play a productive role in society. Daniel Yankelovich conducted national attitude studies of college students from 1968 to 1971 and found that two-thirds of college students profess mainstream views in general. But their feelings in particular about work (and private business) are even more affirmative:

—79% believe that commitment to a meaningful career is a very important part of a person's life.
—85% feel business is entitled to make a profit.
—75% believe it is morally wrong to collect welfare when you can work.
—Only 30% would welcome less emphasis on working hard.

While student feelings about work itself are generally high, Yankelovich found that attitudes toward authority are changing rapidly. In 1968 over half (56%) of all students indicated that they did not mind the future prospect of being "bossed around" on the job. By 1971 only one out of three students (36%) saw themselves willingly submitting to such authority. Equally important, while 86% of these students still believe that society needs some legally based authority to prevent chaos, they nevertheless see a distinction between this necessity and an authoritarian work setting.

Rising Expectations

Yankelovich also found a shift in student opinion on the issue that "hard work will always pay off" from a 69% affirmation in 1968 to a 39% affirmation in 1971. This certainly was, in part, indicative of the conditions in the job market for college graduates in 1971. But more basically, we believe, it highlights a paradox inherent in a populace with increasing educational achievement. Along with the mass media, education and its credentials are raising expectations faster than the economic system can meet them. Much of what is interpreted as antiwork attitudes on the part of youth, then, may be their appraisal of the kinds of jobs that are open to them.

The following case study of a young woman who is a recent college graduate illustrates the gap between expectations and reality:

> I didn't go to school for four years to type. I'm bored; continuously humiliated. They sent me to Xerox school for three hours. . . . I realize that I sound cocky, but after you've been in the academic world, after you've had your own class (as a student teacher) and made your own plans, and someone tries to teach you to push a button—you get pretty mad. They even gave me a goldplated plaque to show I've learned how to use the machine.

The problem is compounded by the number of students who are leaving school with advanced degrees, like the young Chicago lawyer in the following case:

> You can't wait to get out and get a job that will let you do something that's really important. . . . You think you're one of the elite. Then you go to a place like the Loop and there are all these lawyers, accountants, etc., and you realize that you're just a lawyer. No, not even a lawyer—an employee; you have to check in at nine and leave at five. I had lots of those jobs—summers—where you punch in and punch out. You think it's going to be different but it isn't. You're in the rut like everybody else.

Today's youth are expecting a great deal of intrinsic reward from work. Yankelovich found that students rank the opportunity to "make a contribution," "job challenge," and the chance to find "self-expression" at the top of the list of influences on their career choice. A 1960 survey of over 400,000 high school students was repeated for a representative sample in 1970, and the findings showed a marked shift from the students valuing job security and opportunity for promotion in 1960 to valuing "freedom to make my own decisions" and "work that seems important to me" in 1970.

Many of these student findings were replicated in the Survey of Working Conditions sample of young workers. For example, it seems as true of young workers as it is of students that they expect a great deal of fulfillment from work. But the Survey findings show that young workers are not deriving a great deal of satisfaction from the work they are doing. Less than a quarter of young workers reply "very often" when asked the question, "How often do you feel you leave work with a good feeling that you have done something particularly well?"

Age Group	Percentage Answering "Very Often"
Under 20	23
20–29	25
30–44	38
45–64	43
65 and over	53

Other findings document that young workers place more importance on the value of interesting work and their ability to grow on the job than do their elders. Thye also place less importance than do older workers on such extrinsic factors as security and whether or not they are asked to do excessive amounts of work. But the Survey documents a significant gap between the expectations or values of the young workers and what they actually experience on the job. Young workers rate their jobs lower than do older workers on how well their jobs actually live up to the factors they most sought in work. For example, the young value challenging work highly but say that the work they are doing has a low level of challenge.

It has also been found that a much higher percentage of younger than older workers feel that management emphasizes the *quantity* more than the *quality* of their work. Furthermore, it is shown that this adversely affects the satisfaction of younger workers. Such findings contradict the viewpoint that there is a weakening of the "moral fiber" of youth.

Many young union members are challenging some basic assumptions about "a fair day's work for a fair day's pay." In the past, unions concerned themselves with establishing what a fair day's pay would be, while the employer's prerogative was to determine what constitutes a fair day's work. Young workers are now challenging both unions and management by demanding a voice in the setting of both standards, as the following case illustrates:

> Three young workers, aged 20 and 21, were hired to clean offices at night. One evening the foreman caught one of the young janitors (who went to school during the day) doing his homework; another was reading the paper, and the third was asleep with his feet up on a desk. The foreman exploded and gave them a written warning. The workers filed a grievance protesting the warnings: "We cleaned all the offices in five hours by really hustling and who the hell should get upset because we then did our own thing." One young worker said, "At school during study period I get my studies done in less than the hour and no one bugs me when I do other things for the rest of the time. We cleaned all those offices in five hours instead of eight. What more do they want?"

The union steward said he tried hard to understand what they were saying: "But the company has the right to expect eight hours work for eight hours pay. I finally got the kids to understand by taking them outside and telling them that if they got the work finished in five hours, then the company would either give them more work, or get rid of one of them. They're spacing it out nicely now and everyone's happy," he said, satisfied to have settled the grievance within the understood rules.

The author of this study writes that the young workers were far from satisfied with the agreement. They wanted the union to establish what had to be done and how much they would be paid to do it, and then they wanted the same freedom that professionals have to decide how to operate within the time and work frame allotted.

In summary, we interpret these various findings not as demonstrating a shift away from valuing work *per se* among young people, but as a shift away from their willingness to take on meaningless work in authoritarian settings that offers only extrinsic rewards. We agree with Willis Harman that:

> the shape of the future will no more be patterned after the hippie movement and the Youth Revolution than the Industrial Age could have been inferred from the "New Age" values of the Anabaptists.

New Values

A mistake is made, however, if one believes that the new attitudes toward authority and the meaning of work are limited to hippies. Judson Gooding writes that young managers, both graduates of business schools and executive trainees, "reflect the passionate concerns of youth in the 1970s—for individuality, openness, humanism, concern and change—and they are determined to be heard."

Some young people are rejecting the corporate or bureaucratic worlds, while not rejecting work or the concept of work or profit. Gooding tells of one young former executive who quit his job with a major corporation because

> You felt like a small cog. Working there was dehumanizing and the struggle to get to the top didn't seem worth it. They made no effort to encourage your participation. The decisions were made in those rooms with closed doors. . . . The serious error they made with me was not giving me a glimpse of the big picture from time to time, so I could go back

to my little detail, understanding how it related to the whole.

This young man has now organized his own small business and designed his own job. As the publisher of a counterculture newspaper, he might be considered a radical in his beliefs and lifestyle, yet he says "profit is not an evil." Of course, many young workers do question the *use* of profits, especially those profits that they feel are made at the expense of society or the environment. Some businesses themselves are adopting this same attitude.

It may be useful to analyze the views of today's youth not in terms of their parents' values but in terms of the beliefs of their grandparents. Today's youth believe in independence, freedom, and risk —in short, they may have the entrepreneurial spirit of early capitalism. Certainly they are more attracted to small and growing companies, to small businesses and to handicrafts, than to the bureaucracy, be it privately or publicly owned. (The declining opportunity for such small-scale endeavors contributes to dissatisfaction of the young and their apparent lack of commitment to the kinds of jobs that are available.) On the other hand, their parents share a managerial ethic that reflects the need for security, order, and dependence that is born of hard times. Of course, this is being a bit unfair to the older generation and a bit over-generous with our youth, but it serves to get us away from the simplistic thinking that the "Protestant ethic has been abandoned." Who in America ever had the Portestant ethic and when? Did we have it in the thirties? Did the poor people or even middle-class people ever have it? It is argued by Sebastian deGrazia that the Protestant ethic was never more than a myth engendered by the owner and managerial classes to motivate the lower working class—a myth which the latter never fully accepted. Clearly, it is difficult to measure the past allegiance of a populace to an ideology.

But we *can* measure the impact of the present work environment on youth's motivation to work. For example, the Survey of Working Conditions found that youth seem to have a lower attachment to work than their elders on the same job. There are several reasons other than a change in the work ethic why this might be so. *First,* as we have already posited, young people have high expectations generated by their greater education. *Second,* their greater affluence makes them less tolerant of unrewarding jobs. *Third,* many new workers, particularly women, are voluntary workers. They are more demanding because they don't *have* to take a job. *Fourth,* all authority in our society is being challenged—professional athletes challenge owners, journalists challenge editors, consumers challenge manufacturers, the moral authority of religion, nation, and elders is challenged. *Fifth,* many former students are demanding what they achieved in part on their campuses a few years ago—a voice in setting the goals of the organization. The lecture has been *passé* for several years on many campuses—in colloquia and in seminars students challenge teachers. Managers are now facing the products of this progressive education. (One wonders what will happen when the children of today's open classroom, who have been taught to set their own goals and plan their own schedules, enter the workforce.) *Sixth,* young blue-collar workers, who have grown up in an environment in which equality is called for in all institutions, are demanding the same rights and expressing the same values as university graduates. *Seventh,* there is growing professionalism among many young white-collar workers. They now have loyalty to their peer group or to their task or discipline, where once they had loyalty to their work organization.

In sum, it does not appear that young workers have a lower commitment to work than their elders. The problem lies in the interaction between work itself and the changing social character of today's generation, and in the failure of decision makers in business, labor, and government to recognize this fact.

The young worker is in revolt not against work but against the authoritarian system developed by industrial engineers who felt that "the worker was stupid, overly emotional . . . insecure and afraid of responsibility." This viewpoint is summed up in Frederick Taylor's classic dictum to the worker:

> For success, then, let me give one simple piece of advice beyond all others. Every day, year in and year out, each man should ask himself, over and over again, two questions. First, "What is the name of the man I am now working for?" and having answered this definitely, then, "What does this man want me to do, right now?"

The simplistic authoritarianism in this statement would appear ludicrous to the young worker who is not the uneducated and irresponsible person on whom Taylor's system was premised. Yet, many in industry continue to support a system of

motivation that was created in an era when people were willing to be motivated by the stick. As an alternative to this approach, many personnel managers have offered the carrot as a motivator, only to find that young people also fail to respond to this approach.

From our reading of what youth wants, it appears that under current policies, employers may not be able to motivate young workers at all. Instead, employers must create conditions in which the worker can motivate himself. This concept is not as strange as it seems. From biographies of artists, athletes, and successful businessmen, one finds invariably that these people set goals for *themselves.* The most rewarding race is probably one that runs against oneself. Young people seem to realize this. They talk less positively than do their elders about competition with others. But they do talk about self-actualization and other "private" values. Yankelovich found that 40% of students—an increasing percentage—do not believe that "competition encourages excellence," and 80% would welcome more emphasis in the society on self-expression.

Compared to previous generations, the young person of today wants to measure his improvement against a standard he sets for himself. (Clearly, there is much more inner-direction than David Riesman would have predicted two decades ago.) The problem with the way work is organized today is that it will not allow the worker to realize his own goals. Because of the legacy of Taylorism, organizations set a fixed standard for the worker, but they often do not tell him clearly why that standard was set or how it was set. More often than not, the standard is inappropriate for the worker. And, in a strange contradiction to the philosophy of efficient management, the organization seldom gives the worker the wherewithal to achieve the standard. It is as if the runner did not know where the finish line was; the rules make it a race that no worker can win.

It is problematic whether the intolerance among young workers of such poor management signals temporary or enduring changes in the work ethic. More important is how management and society will reckon with the new emphasis that the workplace should lose its authoritarian aura and become a setting for satisfying and self-actualizing activity.

From *Work in America,* Report of a Special Task Force to the United States Secretary of Health, Education, and Welfare. Prepared under the auspices of the W. E. Upjohn Institute for Employment Research (Cambridge, Mass.: The M.I.T. Press, 1973). Reprinted here by permission.

Suggestions For Digging Into The Issue

Discussion Questions

1. How realistic is the expectation that a worker will find real job satisfaction? And can a worker justify putting his best effort into a job when it may not be his real interest in life?

2. Are careers—long-term commitments to a profession or vocation—still possible? Will workers in the future move rapidly from one type of work to another?

3. To what extent is today's generation of young workers imbued with the entrepreneurial spirit?

4. Do you understand work to arise from a religious commitment (as vocation used to be considered a "calling"), or does work now have, universally, a secular meaning?

5. Does it pay in spiritual and psychological terms to work for forty hours a week at a steady job? Compare the tradeoffs made by regular workers between their job and their recreational pursuits, and a person who chooses not to work at all at a paying job.

Survey

Take a survey of teenagers on their attitudes toward work. Some questions can be developed from the article. Then compare your results with the surveys reported on in the article. You might consider using the survey results in preparing questions for a labor leader or corporation manager who could be asked to share views on how "the system" is adapting to young workers.

Career Series

Set up a series of sessions in which different resource persons would be brought in to talk about jobs, professions, and careers. Since most public schools sponsor career days, you could try some angles that are often absent in the school situations. For instance, ask a manager to talk about those who are *not* successful in his business, why they fail, and what a person could do to avoid imitating such failure. Or you might locate a person who has had more than one career and ask him or her to talk about how to make transitions and whether "serial careers" will be the pattern of the future. The religious element can also be included, but probably the most fruitful angle would be an examination of attitudes and values and their origin in basic philosophies and styles of life, rather than asking individuals to speak directly on religion.

Additional Resources

Books listed (many are in paperback) are generally available from bookstores and/or local public libraries. Rental and/or sale prices of other Additional Resource items are available from distributors; their addresses are listed at the back of the book.

Feature Film

Loneliness of the Long Distance Runner (b/w, 103 min. Walter Reade 16). Youth sent to reformatory where he continues his struggle with authority.

Short Films

No Reason to Stay (b/w, 28 min. UCC Office for Audio-Visuals; also McGraw-Hill). Bright student who is "bored to death" in school.

Mr. Grey (color, 10 min. Mass Media). White-collar worker sees himself as a convict.

The Blue Collar Type (color, 51 min. NBC). New breed of worker wants more out of life.

The House That Jack Built (color, 9 min. Learning Corp. of America). Modern conforming man yearns to be different.

Of Time, Work, and Leisure (b/w, 30 min. Mass Media). What happened to the dream that machines would free us for leisure?

Tapes

Working Man (28 min. CSDI #312).

The Crisis of Identity in a Workless World (43 min. CSDI #187).

The Bleak Outlook: Jobs and Machines (50 min. CSDI #78).

The New Breed (29 min. CSDI #313).

Goodbye to the Protestant Ethic (55 min. Pacifica #AL1339).

Working Men (30 min. National Center for Audio Tapes).

Drama

The Interview by Theodore Burtt, Jr. (Contemporary Drama).

Books

Conditions of Labor in American Industries by W. Jett Lauck and Edgar Sydenstricker (New York: Arno Press).

Working People and Their Employers by W. T. Gladden (New York: Arno Press).

Joe Kelly Has Reached His Boiling Point

BY RICHARD ROGIN

On May 8, 1970, construction workers in New York City battled with antiwar demonstrators and two weeks later an estimated one hundred thousand workers marched from City Hall to Battery Park in support of the President's war policies.

Joe Kelly, the subject of this article, was one of the workers. His attitudes and habits provide a rich illustration of how one worker thinks and feels and lives. Joe Kelly is a living example of the lifestyle of an American worker.

Joe Kelly was brought up on Staten Island along with his younger sister, Eileen, who is now a telephone company secretary. His mother had come to America on the boat from County Cavan. His father, who was born in New York, was a paymaster for Esso tankers coming into the port of New York until he died of a heart attack in 1959 at the age of 45.

"My father," Joe Kelly recalls, "used to take me out to the ships on Saturdays to pay off. As a kid they used to let me steer, or let me think I was steering, and let me turn on the radar."

Joe went to elementary and high school at St. Peter's, a parochial school on Staten Island. "I wasn't any angel," he says, "I'm sure of that." He had little trouble passing his subjects and developed a special interest in American history. His major passion, though, was basketball. In high school he played forward on the varsity and was a right-handed pitcher for the baseball team. In the afternoons he delivered *The Staten Island Advance* and worked in a drugstore. He graduated from St. Peter's in 1956 with no specific ambition. He went off to St. Peter's College in Jersey City on a basketball scholarship and lasted a year, passing his courses but admittedly lacking interest in his studies.

With the feeling that he had "had enough school for a while," Joe became a seaman for Mobil Oil for three years. He served on coastal tankers between Texas and Maine and also aboard vessels in the Great Lakes and in New York harbor. Fearful of getting enmeshed in a life he didn't particularly relish, he quit suddenly and enrolled in a night business course at Staten Island's Wagner College. During the day he worked for Coca-Cola, visiting companies that were having trouble balancing their accounts; he hated this job, and left it after a year.

The elevator constructors had just come off a strike in 1960, work was piled up, and some of Joe's friends in the trade asked him if he wanted to come in. Joe says he "jumped at the opportunity" and he is now clearly a man who appreciates his work. His first job, before he was drafted into the Army in 1961, was with a crew automating the elevators at Bergdorf Goodman. When he came out of the service two years later, after enjoying the regimented military life, he went right back to elevators, where he has been ever since.

In 1965 he married a Staten Island girl, Karen Kelsey, who worked as an IBM operator for the Irving Trust Company at 1 Wall. Her father is an office manager for a freight-forwarding concern and, like her, a Republican. Then the children started to arrive and last summer, two days after Joe began what was to become a three-and-a-half-month strike, they moved into their own two-family house. The upstairs six-room apartment is rented to a plumber and his family at $200 a month.

His first big jobs after the Army were in what is called the modernization department of the Otis Elevator Company, for whom he still works—putting automatic elevators in the Municipal Building, in 15 Broad Street, in Con Edison at 14th Street, and in 61 Broadway. Then three or four years ago things began to slow up. "That was about the time," he recalls, "when every Friday the ax was falling and you never knew whether you were gonna have a job Friday afternoon or not." But Joe managed to hang on and he never lost a day because of a layoff. Now elevator constructors talk of a ten-year feast in New York.

Two and a half years ago he was switched to elevator installation and went to work on the General Motors Building. It was his first time on high open steel. "The first morning I will never forget," he says. "The building had just recently been topped out. This was somewhere around the first or second week of January. So when I arrived up on the top of the building, which was about the fifty-second floor, I looked out over the horizon and I saw one of these clocks that flashes the time and the temperature. It was ten minutes after eight and it was minus 2 degrees, and I thought I'd made the biggest mistake of my life."

But he endured the bitter winter cold—and the heights never bothered him. He worked on the TWA terminal at Kennedy Airport on an escalator job, picked up odd electrician's and rigger's jobs during last summer's strike, and late last fall finally became a mechanic after seven long years of apprenticeship as a helper. He started at the World Trade Center, considered the biggest elevator job in the world, just before Christmas.

Until the last two years or so, Joe Kelly had been making about $8,500. Now he is up to $6.86 an hour, and with double pay for the abundant overtime at the Trade Center, he expects to earn between $15,000 and $18,000 this year.

"This is the first year that I've ever made anything like this," he says. "It took ten years to get here, but now I guess I've arrived." He also augments his salary and renting income by bartending three nights a week.

Elevator construction may be well paid, but it is a hard trade and can be dangerous. A good friend of Joe Kelly's, Mike Clancy, 42 years old with five children, plunged twenty-five floors to his death several months ago at the World Trade Center.*

Workers must also beware of tools or material falling from higher stories. "Like if anybody drops anything," says Joe, "they immediately scream, 'Look out below,' and you got to get under something just as quick as you possibly can so it will ricochet off of that instead of off of you."

Joe attends noon Mass on Sundays and he also coaches basketball and baseball teams in a boy's league in Blessed Sacrament parish. (After the Army, he spent three years as a weekend counselor at an orphanage on Staten Island.) His reading consists of *The Daily News*, the *Advance*, the sports section of *The New York Post* and *Popular Mechanics* magazine. The Kellys go out to the movies perhaps every six weeks and may stop in afterward for "a couple of drinks in a nice, quiet, respectable place." Once a week his wife leaves him at home when she goes to play bingo. There is usually a Christmas party for the men on the job, and Otis throws a picnic in the summer. Recently, the elevator constructors and their wives had a $20-a-couple dinner dance at the Commuter's Cafe on Cortlandt Street, across from the Trade Center site. Proceeds from a raffle went to Mike Clancy's family.

On television, Joe enjoys Johnny Cash and Jackie Gleason and sometimes Dean Martin. He likes to be in bed by 11 P.M. Before he was married, Joe played basketball four nights a week in a community-center league. With family responsibilities, his heavy work schedule, and his relative slowness of foot today, he has cut it out completely. "I go down once in a while to watch and eat my heart out," he says.

Joe gets his extravocational workouts now

* In a moving display of the men's strong sense of solidarity, from the young long-haired mod types to grizzled veterans in overalls, more than $18,000 was collected for the Clancy family. Helpers gave $25, mechanics $50, and elevator constructors on other job sites pitched in, as did men in other construction trades. On matters close to the heart—a death on the job, their country in trouble— the men tend to react according to the group working pattern of their trade, en bloc and with great fervor.

around the house, putting in sod, helping to grade the backyard for a large above-ground plastic swimming pool for the children, planting two blue spruces and yews and rhododendrons in the front.

The Kellys haven't been able to take any vacations, though Joe has had two weeks off yearly and will get three weeks under the new contract starting this summer (there was either a strike, or they were saving for the house, or the children were too small). Perhaps twice a summer they drive down to the New Jersey shore around Belmar in their 1967 English Ford station wagon and go swimming.

Why does he work so hard? "A lot of people ask me that," he says. "I wanted the house. Right? I wanted something nice for the wife and the kids, someplace where the kids could grow up and have their own backyard. They wouldn't have to be running out in the street. And now I have the house and I want it fixed up nice. And maybe when it is fixed up nice, I'll relax a bit." Meanwhile, he is at the "boiling point."

My belief is, physical violence doesn't solve a damn thing. One party has to sway the other party to his belief and then the argument is settled. I honestly don't believe that there will be any more physical violence in New York City. I think that one Friday and it's over with. I don't like to see anybody get bounced. I saw some of those kids go down and I didn't think they were gonna get up. I certainly don't agree with them. I would much rather prefer grabbing them by the head of the hair and taking a scissors and cutting their hair off, something that was much less violent but you still would have gotten your message across.

Up at City Hall it became obvious that they had better get that flag back up to the top of the mast. Within a few minutes the flag went back up and everybody seemed nice and happy and again they started singing "God Bless America" and the national anthem and again it made you feel good. Not that I like seeing those four kids out in wherever it was, Kent, get killed. I don't like to see anybody get beat up, never mind lose their life.

I don't think Mayor Lindsay has the right to put that flag at half-staff. That flag represents this country, so the leading representative of the country, who is President Nixon to me, is the only one that has the power or the right to raise or lower a flag.

Joe Kelly says he never even asked what his father's politics were, believing it to be a man's private affair. How did he arrive as a militant member of the no-longer-silent majority? What brought him to believe that Communism was undermining America from within?

"Two people stand out in my mind," Joe says, "why I'm taking part. Joe McCarthy often said, beware of this school system; they're going to infiltrate, brainwash the kids. And Khrushchev in 1960 banging on the UN table. He said they wouldn't have to take over this country physically, they'd do it from within." Though he was only a youngster during McCarthy's heyday, Kelly says: "It's something I've read somewhere along the line." He feels that the students are only dupes in the hands of subversive teachers who, Joe hints, are under the control of foreign powers. In some way, the bad teachers have to be weeded out, he says.

Joe Kelly first voted in 1960, when he chose John F. Kennedy over Nixon for President because he was impressed with Kennedy's performance in the TV debates. Though he still reveres President Kennedy, he wouldn't vote that way again. By 1964 he had swung to the right and voted for Goldwater over Johnson. In the 1965 and 1969 New York mayoral races, he voted the Conservative party line for William F. Buckley, Jr., and John Marchi. He cast his ballot for Nixon for President in 1968.

It was the Goldwater campaign that crystallized Joe's feeling about the war in Vietnam. "I think that it all goes back again, like history repeating itself, to Hitler," he says. "When Hitler kept marching into these countries and, instead of just fighting Hitler's country, you were fighting all these countries after a while. You just can't let Communism take over everything around you because when they got everything around you, they're gonna come after you."

Three men who command his admiration now are John Wayne, Vice-President Agnew, and Chicago Mayor Richard Daley. In fact, Joe wishes New York could borrow Daley for six months to give the city a stiff dose of law and order. He has complete disdain for Mayor Lindsay. He believes Lindsay has turned New York into "welfare city" and is trying to be the champion of welfare recipients and the young antiwar generation in a bid for the Presidency. "Do what you want in Lindsay's city—" he says caustically, "burn the schools. He's got to raise the budget this year to pay for what they burned down."

Of the recent influx of minority workers into his once closely bound union, he says: "They're here to stay, entitled to. But if they're going to work with us, if we go up on the iron and risk our lives walking it, by God, they have to go along with us. There've been several instances in the city where they've refused because they didn't have to."

As for a black family living on his street, he is adamantly against it, feeling that panic-selling would drive down the value of his property. "I had to bust my backside for five years to get that down payment for that house," he says. "I am not interested in seeing all that go down the drain."

It is on this precious ground—his home and his family—that he takes a defiant, mildly worried stand. He would like his daughters to go to college or nursing school and his son to get as much schooling as possible, to become a doctor or a lawyer—"something where he can use his head to make a living, not his back like his old man does."

While his wife hopes and prays that her daughters will never wear their hair straight and long like the hippies and that her children's minds will be protected in parochial schools despite the danger of lay teachers, Joe Kelly tells a story about a neighbor's friend's son, a boy of sixteen.

"This boy," he says, "came home from school one day and he told his father he was a bum, that he was part of the Establishment. And this fellow was a World War II veteran, decorated several times and wounded twice. And he just turned around and he gave the kid a good whack and I guess he broke his jaw or broke his nose and the father was in a turmoil. This is his own flesh and blood talking to him.

"I cannot imagine having my kids come home

and tell me I'm a bum because I believe in the Establishment—and there is nobody that believes in the Establishment more than I do. The more I see of this stuff, the closer I try to become to my kids. I believe that my way is correct, the Establishment way, law and order first, and this is what I'm gonna do my damndest to breed into them so that they don't get some other off-the-wall ideas."

Joe says that if his children ever call him a bum because he believes in the flag, they'd better leave his house. "I would do everything to control myself not to hit them. I mean, this is what I brought into the world. But it's awful hard. I certainly can see that man flying off the handle and whacking the kid. Oh, yeah, he certainly did regret it. But his big question is, Where did his kid get this trend of thinking?"

Joe Kelly doesn't believe that melees such as the memorable one at noon on May 8 are any solution. So his answer, he says reflectively, is to arm himself with education, engage in dialogue.

"When they throw a point at you," he says, "be able to talk to them on their theories on socialism, Communism. This is the best way—to talk them out of the stuff instead of just saying it's un-American or using your fists."

Ironically, Mayor Lindsay has said much the same: "Perhaps their [the construction workers'] demonstrations, in the end, will help us break through to a new dialogue in which we not only talk, but listen."

This article appeared originally in The New York Times, June 28, 1970, and was subsequently published in Overcoming Middle Class Rage by Murray Friedman (Philadelphia: Westminster Press, 1971). It is reprinted here by permission.

Suggestions For Digging Into The Issue

Discussion Questions

1. Would you consider Kelly representative of American workers in his patriotic views? Do you find these views agreeable to your own?

2. How do you respond to Kelly as a human being? What does this human portrait say about stereotypes of workers: blue-collar, ethnic, etc.

3. How do you feel about Kelly's views on work?

4. Would you consider Kelly a racist? For what reasons do you or do you not think so?

5. How can students, intellectuals, minority members, and others establish a dialogue with workers like Kelly? Or would you take the view of some that dialogue is meaningless and that basic changes in the social structure are required before the anger of workers is defused?

Symposium on Ethnics

Ask representatives of a variety of ethnic groups in your community to share in a symposium on different styles among ethnics. These persons might not be members of official organizations but merely individuals with a strong sense of their ethnic identity. Ask each one to talk about the distinctiveness of his or her background and why he or she feels attached to it.

Another symposium approach is to make up a panel—include blacks, WASPs, and others—to talk about the new sense of ethnic identity. Perhaps members of the panel could be given the article on Joe Kelly to read before the session. Then ask each to be prepared to comment on whether they consider ethnic pride a positive force and whether ethnics' sense of being trodden on is justified.

Street Festival

Have a street festival in your neighborhood or community to give ethnics a chance to display their cultural heritage. You could have booths like they have at carnivals, or simply arrange for bands, artists' displays, and dancing as a way of celebrating diversity.

Encounter

If you feel up to it, arrange a discussion between an articulate blue-collar worker who might represent an attitude and values like those of Joe Kelly and a young person representing the counterculture. Ask them to talk about patriotism as a value and what should be done to change or preserve certain social values.

Additional Resources

Books listed (many are in paperback) are generally available from bookstores and/or local public libraries. Rental and/or sale prices of other Additional Resource items are available from distributors; their addresses are listed at the back of the book.

Feature Film

Joe (b/w, 115 min. Cannon). Focuses on hardhat laborer burning to gun down hippies.

Short Films

Assembly Line (b/w, 27 min. UCC Office for Audio-Visuals; also Mass Media). Worker finds the weekend as sterile and lonely as the assembly line.

Jobs and Advancement: On the Move (color, 17 min. Indiana Univ.). Dramatizes need for and recommends methods of achieving upward mobility in world of work.

Tapes

The Neglected White Worker (26 min. CSDI #514).

Labor Looks at Itself (29 min. CSDI #37R).

TV

All in the Family (see TV Guide or newspaper listings for local stations and time).

Books

Blue Collar Worker: A Symposium on Middle America (New York: McGraw-Hill).

The Laborer: A Remedy for His Wrongs by W. Dealtry (New York: Arno Press).

The Christian Style of Life: Problematics of a Good Idea

BY JAMES M. GUSTAFSON

What might it mean to talk about a "style of life"? The idea has had some currency in Christian discourse in recent years, both in the United States and abroad. The word "style" has several uses that might pertain to the Christian life. One is a descriptive use; a style of life would be comparable to a style of art. There are certain common characteristics of artistic expression that enable the observer to make a roughly valid generalization pertaining to an "impressionist" style, or a "non-representational" style. To the person somewhat literate in the arts, such adjectives modifying "style" enable him to prejudge or to classify in his mind the work he has not yet seen, or has just seen. Thus when men write about a "Christian" style of life, they may seem to refer to a descriptive generalization;[1] there are presumably sufficient visible or audible characteristics of the behavior of Christians for one to in some measure predict what the behavior of Christians will be, or to classify behavior that is observed as belonging to a class called Christian. We shall return to this kind of usage subsequently.

A second usage is a qualitative one. In common speech we say of one performer that he has "style," or of a political figure that he has or lacks "style." What we mean is that there is a quality of excellence that defies precise description, but nonetheless exists in the manner of performance or manner of life that we observe. The judgment is qualitative, though elements of a normative description[2] are obviously involved. To justify a judgment that one man has "style" and another lacks it, we usually engage in comparative descriptions, and hope that in the process the grounds for the claim will become evident. Thus when used in Christian discourse, men may wish to suggest that what some Christians have and others ought to have is Christian *style*, that is, a quality of excellence in the way that they live the Christian life. The judgment about whether a Christian has style or not is probably much like the aesthetic judgment made about a work of art; there are some accepted canons for rational discrimination, but other things are also involved, such as our affective capabilities, our sensibilities and sensitivities. In judging the style, we assume that not all persons will agree on the proper evaluation, though we hope for some consensus. Whereas all informed men can agree on the correct answer to a mathematical problem, informed men will not agree on what excellence is in the performance of the Christian life.

I suspect that when writers use "Christian style of life" they intend a combination of the descriptive and the evaluative uses of the word. I also suspect that in some very popular discourse the term is used more because it has evocative and persuasive power for some audiences, rather than because it has clear and precise references. For some persons the term has a glorious ambiguity in which they relish; in this chapter my intention is to show that it can be explicated more clearly without losing its suggestive richness.

Does a descriptive usage make sense? Are there common "Christian" characteristics of life that form a class of behavior or of persons? To answer this, we need to make more precise what we are looking for. If we can sort out what things we might look for, we are making some progress. Do we expect most Christians to do the same kinds of things in similar circumstances? Perhaps under certain circumstances we could expect more, and others less. In situations analogous to that of the Good Samaritan we might expect Christians to behave in a manner similar to his deeds. On a question of the proper zoning of an urban community, we would not expect as many Christians to have the same opinion or behave in the same way. Presumably the Christian "style" in the first instance would be deeds that meet the concrete physical and spiritual needs of a stranger or a neighbor regardless of the inconvenience to the self. We might predict that conscientious Christians would "do something like that"; when we see it done, we are likely to call it a "Christian" act. If a person goes through life very consistently living as a Good Samaritan, we might judge that his life had a style. If an identifiable religious group has such characteristic ways of acting, we might use the word "style" to describe its corporate life. Perhaps there is a Quaker Christian style, for example.

More than a man's faith goes into such a style; his sensitivity to suffering and injustice may be governed more by his own experience of suffering and injustice than it is by a recollection that God made himself known in Jesus Christ through costly love. He may be brought up in a family that for various reasons has nourished a sensitivity that leads to self-sacrificial deeds. Perhaps his family has some inner historical connection with a people who have been persecuted or deprived through centuries of life: Jews, Anabaptists, Negroes. Perhaps there is a family ethos rooted in part in deeply individual response to either tenderness expressed by parents, or in reaction to having not known affection and concern that stimulates deeds of sacrificial love. One might, however, make a case that a Good Samaritan style is consistent with conscientious Christian loyalty, and that such a normative description can inform those who are disposed by other factors to behave in such a way. For some men, their Christian faith may provide more "justifying reasons" than motivating ones to life in a certain way. For others perhaps their faith motivates as well as justifies and directs their Good Samaritan style.

Would a Good Samaritan style become a test of Christian behavior? Certainly it ought not become a test of Christian *faith* in the sense of trust. But would we be willing to say that those who have the Good Samaritan style show more integrity concerning faith and action than those who do not? Probably not, since there are other styles that are consistent (maybe just as consistent) with Christian faith. Perhaps there is a militant style of Christian life which does not rest with acts of personal love, but moves into the battles between better and worse, between greater justice and gross injustice with more boldness than humility, with the armor of demonstrations on the streets provoking tension, rather than the medical service of binding the wounds of those who suffer strains and stresses caused by social struggles. Such a style also could be motivated by more or by other than loyalty to Christ. Perhaps there is a free style of Christian life; indeed, such seems to be somewhat in vogue at the present time among some Christians. The life pattern expressed in behavior is a care-lessness, a demonstration in heedless behavior and iconoclastic words and deeds to show that to be a Christian is to be unbound by conventions that oppressive social customs present to

one. It is to recall that "all things are lawful" even though it may be to forget that "not all things are helpful." Again, perhaps more or other than a Christian loyalty governs such a style; it may be evoked by the dreadful boredom that conventionally responsible and respectable people seem to live by.

Descriptive usages of "Christian style of life" with reference to visible behavior need to be exercised with caution. Perhaps at best there are "Christian styles" of life on this level. There can be individual and communal patterns of behavior in the world that have consistency enough to be called styles. But what we observe may be motivated by allegiance to Christ as this allegiance directs and strengthens tendencies arising from social experiences or individual experiences. One would also have to inquire whether the consistency of behavior cannot be broken; the militant Christian freedom rider may be on another occasion the Franciscan binder of wounds, and on another the rebellious challenger of prevailing modes of Christian respectability. Or different historical events might legitimately evoke a communal style that is ephemeral; in a time of civil rights crisis a more militant style may be evoked among the churches; in another crisis another style may be visible. And finally, perhaps within the Christian community various styles can coexist at the same time; to judge the rightness of this is to raise the normative qualitative question, a question deferred for the moment.

But "style" may refer to characteristic dispositions and attitudes of Christians, rather than to highly visible deeds, though attitude and deed are related. Is there a style of Christian disposition that can be descriptively determined? Can we talk with thousands of Christians and then formulate a generalization about the "Christian attitude" toward life, or the world? What kinds of things might we look for? As a starting point we would ask about the Christian virtues, as these might be transposed into dispositional terms. Are Christians hopeful? We might say normatively that they *ought* to be hopeful, for there is a consistency between trust in God's graciousness and a disposition of hopefulness. If we found hopeful Christians, could we assess to what extent their hopefulness was a correlate of their faith and to what extent it was the result of personal experiences with other people that assured them that the possibilities of life are more manifold and powerful than its threats? And, one would wonder whether some hopeful persons are not deluded, living in a world of unreality and sheltered from evil.

Are Christians loving? It would seem that their faith ought to engender a disposition to be loving. "For God is love." "If God so loved us, we also *ought* to love one another." "We love, because he first loved us." We could make loving more explicit by suggesting with H. R. Niebuhr that love is rejoicing in the presence of the beloved; it is gratitude, reverence and loyalty toward him. The existence of attitudes like these might be inferred from actions that demonstrate joy, gratitude, respect, and fidelity. Or we might detect such dispositions in the gestures and words of men. But such dispositions may come about as much by having loving parents, as by trusting in God's love. "Perfect love casts out fear." This could be a descriptive statement as used by the author of I John. If it is, we ought to find dispositions in Christians, if they are in God's love, that are free from anxieties, that give an equanimity of spirit and soul. But, again, not all peaceful souls are identified with the Christian community; some men achieve inner calm by breathing exercises and some by drugs. And not all Christians have an inner peace; many are anguished about the world, the credibility of their belief and the goodness of God, not to mention where their bread for the morrow will come from.

If a Christian style refers to a set of dispositions, or to what Paul calls the gifts of the Spirit, we might draw some profile of what some Christians are, others can become, and perhaps all ought to be. But quickly one has moved from the descriptive to the normative. And since such motivations as may come from a graced and trusting Christian belief enter in confluence with many other experiences, some measure of latitude and flexibility will always be called for if one wishes to risk generalizations about a "style" that refers to dispositions and attitudes.

One may wish to say less about achieved behavior and persisting actual dispositions, and say more about the *intentions* of Christians. The "style" may be more intentional than visibly actual. But care needs to be taken in formulating such a generalization. Are we talking about existing intentions among conscientious Christians or about intentions that Christians ought to have? All the qualifications and pluralisms that can be brought to bear on descriptive generalizations about behavior and attitudes can be brought to bear on intentions.

It becomes clear that when we are talking about a Christian style of life we are speaking qualitatively, both about a pattern of life that we could develop in normative descriptions, and about the intensity and seriousness with which that style might be manifest in the intentions, attitudes, and behavior of Christians. We cannot assess the behavior of Christians, or their attitudes and intentions, and give a descriptive generalization about a style of life that *thereby* becomes normative.

When we turn to the normative, we are confronted with at least as much complexity as we are in thinking in descriptive terms. Three areas of complication deserve attention here. Where do we find the normative style? How do we talk about it in such a way as to avoid "pursuit of ideals" and other theologically problematic terms? How are "styles" as norms embodied in behavior as visible and actual?

Certainly Christians in our generation have been reluctant to talk about normative style for many reasons. One is that we do not know how to decide between styles. The inner-worldly asceticism of the Troeltsch-Weber interpretation has been an actual style that for many reasons undergoes criticism now.[3] It referred basically to attitude, but also to intention and to acts. Now we are counseled to a worldly holiness, or to a secular style, which again may be more attitudinal than visible according to a behavioral norm. When we write about a Christian style, perhaps it is best even at the normative level to be pluralistic— Christian styles of life.* We can argue for better or worse styles being more or less appropriate to the changing times on the one hand, and the continuing faith on the other. But pluralism[4] is necessary whether we consider the matter historically, or as a contemporary issue.

Saints and Jesus

To look at the matter historically requires a kind of study that Protestants have seldom pursued; namely, of the biographies of Christians and the history of conduct of Christian groups, those declared saints and those undeclared saints, those communities that were monastic and those communities that were inner-worldly ascetic. What can we learn from a John Wollman and a John Winthrop, a John Bunyan and a John Calvin?[5] Is a "Quaker style" important to keep in view not

* See my "Types of Moral Life," *Religious Education*, 57 (November–December, 1962), 403–410.

only as theologically legitimate, but historically effective as a mediation of God's grace and order? Is a "Puritan style" equally important and legitimate? What is right and wrong about Russian spirituality, about Franciscan style, about Saint Birgitta of Sweden or Joan of Arc?[6] How have styles that might contribute to a normative description been related to their historical occasions and their Christian forms of piety? No historical movement or figure would give us the pattern for today; yet there may be wisdom in looking to history for a way of thinking analogically about what style ought to be nourished in our time.

Protestants are more experienced at biblical than historical study. But there too is plurality. I read I Peter as accenting a kind of submissiveness as an appropriate attitude under certain circumstances. I read I John as a great testimony to God's love and man's loving possibilities. I read Galatians as a testimony to Christian liberty. Not all three can necessarily be harmonized in one man at one time; not all three may be appropriate on the same occasion. Perhaps the Christian community needs persons and groups angular enough to stress one to the neglect of others, to remind the whole body of the ministries of various of its members.

The apostolic accounts of the life and teachings of Jesus are bound to be perused for some purposes of contemporary normative usage. One need be neither a biblical literalist nor a romantic idealist to see the coherence between the faith in the love and trustworthiness of God that Jesus preached and the sayings and deeds with which the gospel writers credit him. If it is meaningful to speak about a Christian style of life at all, one must assume that a consistency is possible between trust and belief in Jesus Christ on the one hand, and man's intentions, dispositions, and actions on the other. To say that the perennial attractiveness of Jesus Christ arises in part out of the consistency between his faith in God and his life is not to say that is the only significance that he has. But it is to suggest that the Christian community does have a model, a norm, in relation to which all historical styles can be evaluated, and by which all can be informed. What does imitation or discipleship of him mean? This is always a proper question to ask in forming a view of a proper pattern of Christian life. It is not easily answered, as one sees in the history of Christian morality and spirituality. For some the deeds and works become the new law, more extrinsic and literal than the Holy Spirit in the heart. For others

the key is the kind of relationship between God and man and between man and man that one sees there. For others Christians are to have attitudes that are like the attitudes toward others that are portrayed in the narratives and speeches. There is always also the problem of finding the ways to express that discipleship in the present culture, with its modern modes and morals.

But the sources of insight into norm need never be mechanically sought; clearly the imagination and sensibilities of men are important in expression of faith and lifestyles. As Mrs. Sallie TeSelle indicates in her book, *Literature and the Christian Life* (New Haven: Yale University Press, 1966), the concreteness of not only the parable in the gospels, but of imaginative literature, can function to stimulate imagination and concreteness in the lives of Christians.

Can we talk about normative styles without falling into theological pitfalls? Lutherans have been, in this non-Lutheran writer's judgment, particularly sensitive to certain problems at this point. The main one is the temptation to confuse the shaping of life in accord with one's belief with the attainment of grace and God's righteousness. Many others have been concerned to avoid the Charles Sheldon[7] type of idealization, in which the Christian life is both the striving to approximate ideals and the wooden unimaginative application of them to human affairs. I confine myself to an assertion. When we speak of norms in the context of the Christian life, we are assuming the richness of the divine beneficence, the empowering and guiding new life given by the Spirit, and are only concerned with a matter of high order practicality; namely, what shape ought life under the impact of human decisions and actions take so that it is more in accord with that beneficence and that new life.

The Shaping of Life

Finally, how do "styles" normatively described become embodied in words and deeds? By God's graces and guidance, yes, but not without conforming and confirming thoughts and deeds of men. Here I only suggest that we need to think more clearly about how men's lives are shaped. Aristotle tells us the obvious; namely, that men become lyre players by playing the lyre, and builders by building. Werner Jaeger makes clear that while the normative styles changed in ancient Greece, *paideia*[8] was present in every place and time. I mean to suggest that we need to explore the significance of conscious intention to shape a life in accord with God's good will, and of the practice it takes to become a fitting living active person conforming life to God's goodness. We need to explore what forms the conscience, what centers bring life to wholeness and integrity and "style," what brings lasting dispositions into being that give order and direction to gesture, word, and deed.

We do not have the cohesiveness of earlier isolated city-states or of Christendom. We have pluralism in culture as well as vast individual differences. Such observations are commonplace. But such commonplaces make no less important the task of each Christian being shaped in all his idiosyncrasies and commonalities by his confirmation of and conformation with the grace and will of God. Each Christian will have his style. Nor do such commonplaces vitiate the concern for guidance in communities. We need to see more clearly the style of Christian life that helps us conform our culture and society, our time and place to the grace and will of God. And we need to generously acknowledge that in the sovereignty of God's grace, there are many members to Christ's body, and not all have the same function. There will be the healers and the disturbers, the aggressive and the timid, those identified with the "secular" and those concerned to preserve the integrity of the tradition, the Schweitzers, the Reinhold Niebuhrs,[9] and countless more.

This article appeared originally in *Una Sancta,* 24, 1 (1967) and was subsequently published in *Christian Ethics and the Community* by James M. Gustafson (Philadelphia: United Church Press, 1971). It is reprinted here by permission.

Editor's Notes to "The Christian Style of Life"

1. A descriptive generalization, in ethics, is a statement that explains actions from a more or less neutral standpoint. For example, one could say, "Christians very often go to church," or "Wars involve the deaths of large numbers of people."

2. A normative description, in ethics, is a statement that calls for a rule or standard that a group applies to itself. For example: "Christians love their neighbors." This statement describes the behavior of some Christians. It also implies an "ought"—that Christians should love if they are truly Christian.

3. Asceticism means to deny the world. Both Ernst Troeltsch (1865–1923) and Max Weber (1864–1920) wrote about the Protestant ethic, which valued self-denial at the same time it encouraged persons to make money.

4. Pluralism means more than a society with groups that have different points of view. It implies the central values of these groups are on the same level.

5. John Woolman, the usual spelling (1720–1772), was an American Quaker who crusaded against slavery. John Winthrop (1588–1649) was Puritan leader of the Massachusetts Bay Colony and emphasized the providence of God. John Bunyan (1628–1688) was an English Puritan and author of *Pilgrim's Progress.* John Calvin (1509–1564) was the influential Protestant reformer.

6. Birgitta, or Bridget (about 1303–1373), founded the Brigittines order, for men and women, in the Roman Catholic Church. The present communities are made up entirely of women. Joan of Arc (about 1412–1431) felt called by God to lead the French against the English in the Hundred Years War; she was captured, sold to the English, judged a heretic, and burned at the stake.

7. Charles Sheldon (1857–1946) was a Protestant whose book *In His Steps,* a best seller in the 1920s, was based on the idea of modeling the Christian life after Jesus' example.

8. *Paideia* is a Greek term meaning education, or the formation of character by the ideals of culture.

9. Albert Schweitzer (1875–1965) gave up a professorship in Germany and served as a medical doctor in Africa, following his concept of "reverence for life." Reinhold Niebuhr (1892–1971) was a foremost thinker in Protestant ethics who emphasized the activist life of Christians in society.

Suggestions For Digging Into The Issue

Discussion Questions

1. What do these phrases mean to you as descriptions of a possible Christian style: the Good Samaritan? the militant? the free styles?

2. Why is it always difficult to measure faith, love, loyalty, and other intangible realities?

3. What are the dangers in saying one style or form of behavior is Christian and another is not? Can some forms of behavior be ruled unchristian under any circumstances—expressions of racial prejudice, for example, or killing?

4. How true to Jesus do you think the Jesus people or Jesus freaks are?

5. Could it be said that Christians should be more insistent than others on a pluralistic approach to alternate lifestyles—that individuals and groups should have the right to express themselves in any style of their choosing?

6. Are there styles of life that more nearly capture a Christian quality of life than do others? If so, what are they?

Directed Reading

Ask a mature young person or an adult to study the article before a session. At the session, the leader can outline the article or call attention to several sentences in it that are important. The leader may want to write the outline or sentences on a chalkboard, newsprint, or transparency for overhead projection. Or if several copies of the book are available, the leader can simply ask group members to underline sentences as the article is gone through. After going through the article in this way for ten to fifteen minutes, the group can take each sentence or idea by itself and discuss it.

For example, some significant sentences from the article seem to be:

"Thus when men write about a 'Christian' style of life, they may seem to refer to a descriptive generalization. . . ." (Here the leader may want to define the meaning of "descriptive" in this sense.)

"A second usage is a qualitative one."

"But 'style' may refer to characteristic dispositions and attitudes of Christians, rather than to highly visible deeds, though attitude and deed are related."

"One may wish to say less about achieved behavior and persisting actual dispositions, and say more about the *intentions* of Christians."

"When we write about a Christian style, perhaps it is best even at the normative level to be pluralistic —Christian styles of life."

Some of these technical ethical terms are defined in *Christian Word Book* (Abingdon Press, 1968) or other handbooks and dictionaries of religious terms.

Bible Study

Take several Bible passages that suggest a particular way of acting or living as a total response on the part of the faithful. Look at the passage carefully, use a commentary for additional information and try to determine if the passage indicates a distinctive quality that must always be a part of the life of faith. Such passages might include the parable of the Good Samaritan (Luke 10:30–37), the parable of the Last Judgment (Matthew 25:31–46), and the "love" chapter of I Corinthians (Chapter 13).

Panel

Consider assembling a panel of persons representing a variety of religious styles, such as the activist, mystic, academic, and revivalist. Ask each panel member to respond to some of the questions listed under "Discussion Questions." See if the panel can help answer the question whether there is a Christian style of life, or *styles* of life.

Additional Resources

Books listed (many are in paperback) are generally available from bookstores and/or local public libraries. Rental and/or sale prices of other Additional Resource items are available from distributors; their addresses are listed at the back of the book.

Feature Films

Heavens Above (b/w, 118 min. Audio/Brandon). Episcopal priest seeks to be true Christian minister in modern church.

Monsieur Vincent (subtitles, b/w, 112 min. Audio/Brandon). Seventeenth-century priest who traveled throughout France helping poor and diseased and teaching Christian love.

The Gospel According to Matthew (subtitles, b/w, 136 min. Audio/Brandon). Extremely well-done, literal portrayal of Jesus of Matthew's gospel by a Communist director.

Nazarin (subtitles, b/w, 92 min. Audio/Brandon). Priest in nineteenth century who tries to live by Christ's precepts.

Diary of a Country Priest (subtitles, b/w, 116 min. Audio/Brandon). Story of dying priest who believes he failed, but dies with the understanding, "All is Grace!"

Jesus Christ Superstar (color, 108 min. Universal). From the Broadway musical portrayal of the man Jesus.

Godspell (color, 90 min. Columbia). From the off-Broadway musical portrayal of Jesus of Matthew's gospel, against New York City setting.

Midnight Cowboy (color, 113 min. UA 16). Depicts bond two people form to counteract world's harshness.

Short Films

Parable (color, 22 min. UCC Office for Audio-Visuals; also Mass Media). Communicates discipleship and Christian style of life.

Behold All Things New (color, 30 min. UCC Office for Audio-Visuals; also BFC-TV Films). 1968 Assembly of World Council of Churches captures on film a spirit of hope for a new world.

The World Is Celebration, Parts 1 and 2 (color, 30 min. BFC-TV Films). Part 1: contemporary liturgical experiment; Part 2: congregation experimenting with an encounter happening.

A Thousand Days (b/w, 25 min. Mass Media). Presidential career of John F. Kennedy commemorated.

The String Bean (b/w with color, 17 min. Mass Media). Affirmation of life as portrayed by old lady who nurtures a string bean.

Records

Godspell (Bell #1102).

Jesus Christ Superstar (2 records, Decca #DXSA-7206).

Are You Running with Me, Jesus? (Columbia #CL2548).

A Man Dies (EMI Records #33XX1609).

Drama

That Kook, J.C. by Kris Rosenberg (C6ntemporary Drama).

Books

Mr. Blue by Myles Connolly (Garden City, N.Y.: Doubleday, Image Books).

Jonathan Livingston Seagull by Richard Bach (New York: Macmillan).

Periodicals

D. M. Williams, "Close-up of the Jesus People," in *Christian Century*, August 27, 1971.

B. Vaclor, "Jesus Movement Is Upon Us," in *Look*, February 9, 1971.

Addresses of Distributors

More Sources and Resources

AEVAC
1604 Park Avenue
Plainfield, N.J. 07060

American Documentary Films
336 West 84th Street
New York, N.Y. 10024

Anti-Defamation League of B'nai B'rith
315 Lexington Avenue
New York, N.Y. 10016

Association Films
69 West Washington
Chicago, Ill. 60602

Audio/Brandon Films
34 MacQuesten Parkway South
Mount Vernon, N.Y. 10550

BFC—TV Films
Room 860
475 Riverside Drive
New York, N.Y. 10027

Caedmon Records
505 Eighth Avenue
New York, N.Y. 10018

Cannon Group Incorporated
405 Park Avenue
New York, N.Y. 10022

CBS Television
51 West 52nd Street
New York, N.Y. 10019

Center for Cassette Studies
8110 Webb Avenue
North Hollywood, Calif. 91605

Centron Educational Films
1621 West Ninth Street
Lawrence, Kans. 66044

Cinema 5
595 Madison Avenue
New York, N.Y. 10022

Civic Education Service
1733 K Street, NW
Washington, D.C. 20006

Columbia Pictures
711 Fifth Avenue
New York, N.Y. 10022

Contemporary Drama
Box 457
Downess Grove, Ill. 60515

Creative Visuals
Box 1911
Big Spring, Tex. 79720

CSDI—Center for the Study of
    Democratic Institutions
P.O. Box 4446
Santa Barbara, Calif. 93101

Current Affairs Films
527 Madison Avenue
New York, N.Y. 10022

Denoyer-Groppert
523 Westwood Avenue
Chicago, Ill. 60604

Dynamic Design
1433 N. Central Park Avenue
Anaheim, Calif. 92802

Educational Dimensions Corp.
Box 146
Great Neck, N.Y. 11023

EMI
20 East Huron Street
Chicago, Ill. 60611

Films, Inc.
P.O. Box 11707
Atlanta, Ga. 30305

German Consulate General
535 Boylston Street
Boston, Mass. 02116

Guidance Associates
Pleasantville, N.Y. 10570

Henk Newenhouse
1825 Willow Road
Northfield, Ill. 60093

Human Development Institute
166 East Superior Street
Chicago, Ill. 60111

Impact Films
144 Bleecker Street
New York, N.Y. 10012

Indiana University
Audio-Visual Center
Bloomington, Ind. 47401

Interact
Box 262
Lakeside, Calif. 92040

Janus Films
745 Fifth Avenue
New York, N.Y. 10022

Lead Industries Assn.
292 Madison Avenue
New York, N.Y. 10017

Learning Corporation of America
711 Fifth Avenue
New York, N.Y. 10022

Mass Media Ministries
2116 N. Charles Street
Baltimore, Md. 21218

McGraw-Hill Films
1221 Avenue of the Americas
New York, N.Y. 10036

Media Plus
60 Riverside Drive (Suite 11d)
New York, N.Y. 10024

Miller-Brody Productions, Inc.
342 Madison Avenue
New York, N.Y. 10017

Modern School Supply
524 East Jackson Street
Goshen, Ind. 46526

National Center for Audio Tapes
Bureau of Audio Visual Instruction
University of Colorado
Stadium Building (Room 320)
Boulder, Colo. 80302

NBC Educational Enterprises
30 Rockefeller Plaza
New York, N.Y. 10020

Pacifica Tape Library
2217 Shattuck Avenue
Berkeley, Calif. 94704

Paulist Productions
400 Sette Drive
Paramus, N.J. 07652

Pitman Publishing Corporation
6 East 43rd Street
New York, N.Y. 10017

Pyramid Films
Box 1048
Santa Monica, Calif. 90404

rbc Films
933 North La Brea Avenue
Los Angeles, Calif. 90038

Scholastic Magazines, Inc.
50 West 44th Street
New York, N.Y. 10036

Scott Education Division
Scott Graphics
Holyoke, Mass. 01040

SMCP—Saint Mary's College Press
Christian Brothers Publications
Winona, Minn. 55987

Society for Visual Education
1345 Diversey Parkway
Chicago, Ill. 60614

Teaching Resources
100 Boylan Street
Boston, Mass. 02116

Theme Productions
Detroit, Mich.

Time-Life Films
43 West 16th Street
New York, N.Y. 10011

UCC—United Church of Christ
Office for Audio-Visuals
600 Grand Avenue
Ridgefield, N.J. 07657

OR: 512 Burlington Avenue
     La Grange, Ill. 60525

United Artists 16
729 Seventh Avenue
New York, N.Y. 10019

United Methodist Board of Missions
Service Center
475 Riverside Drive
New York, N.Y. 10027

United Presbyterian Church in the U.S.A.
Witherspoon Building
Philadelphia, Pa. 19107

Universal Pictures
445 Park Avenue
New York, N.Y. 10022

University of Southern California
Department of AV Services
University Park
Los Angeles, Calif. 90007

Walter Reade 16
241 East 34th Street
New York, N.Y. 10016

Warner Bros. Picture Distributing Corp.
666 Fifth Avenue
New York, N.Y. 10019

Warren Schloat Productions
Pleasantville, N.Y. 10570

Western Publishing Co.
850 Third Avenue
New York, N.Y. 10022

Basic Media Resources References

LEARNING DICTIONARY. Westinghouse Learning Corp., 100 Park Avenue, New York, N.Y. 10017. (Comprehensive multimedia resource listings alphabetized by subjects in a set of volumes with yearly supplements.)

NICEM INDEXES. National Information Center for Educational Media, University of Southern California, University Park, Los Angeles, Calif. 90007. (Comprehensive listing of resources in separate volumes by media—one on each medium—for example: Film Index, Filmstrip Index, Video Tape Index.)

MEDIA ONE and MEDIA TWO FOR CHRISTIAN FORMATION. George Pflaum, 38 West Fifth Street, Dayton, Ohio 45402. (Two volumes listing selected individual media resources with descriptions and critiques.)

THE GUIDE TO SIMULATION GAMES FOR EDUCATION AND TRAINING by Paul Twelker. Information Resources, 1675 Massachusetts Avenue, Cambridge, Mass. 02138. (Concise summary descriptions of large number of commercial educational games.)

NATIONAL CENTER FOR AUDIO TAPES CATALOG. Bureau of Audio Visual Instruction, University of Colorado, Boulder, Colo. 80302. (Comprehensive listing of available audio tapes in the U.S.)

SCHWANN RECORD CATALOG. W. Schwann, 134 Newbury Street, Boston, Mass. 02116. (Monthly listings of new and currently available commercial recordings.)

TV Program Information

TV GUIDE. Box 400, Radnor, Pa. 19088. (Weekly schedule and descriptions of television programs.)

TELEVISION INFORMATION OFFICE. 745 Fifth Avenue, New York, N.Y. 10022. (Monthly listing of TV "specials.")

Film Information

CATHOLIC FILM NEWSLETTER. Division for Film and Broadcasting of the U.S. Catholic Conference, Suite 4200, 405 Lexington Avenue, New York, N.Y. 10017. (Monthly descriptions and evaluations of current feature films.)

THEMES: SHORT FILMS FOR DISCUSSION by William Kuhns. George Pflaum, 38 West Fifth Street, Dayton, Ohio 45402. (Descriptions and discussion questions for large number of selected short films.)

AUDIO-VISUAL RESOURCE GUIDE ed. Nick Abrams. Friendship Press annual, 475 Riverside Drive, New York, N.Y. 10027. (Reviews and evaluations on a very wide range of materials that can be used in a variety of religious settings.)

Slide Series

DISCOVERY THROUGH SIGHT. Paulist Press, 400 Sette Drive, Paramus, N.J. 07652. (Two hundred professional slides which can be variously combined for use with any subject.)

MARK IV PRESENTATIONS. La Salette Center, Attleboro, Mass. 02703. (Similar to Discovery series [see above] in usability, but different individual slides.)

Filmstrips

The following are distributors of unusually well-made filmstrips on a variety of current issues:

THOMAS KLISE, Box 3418, Peoria, Ill. 61614.

ARGUS COMMUNICATIONS, 7440 North Natchez Avenue, Niles, Ill. 60648.

GUIDANCE ASSOCIATES, Pleasantville, N.Y. 10570.

Photos

GEORGE PFLAUM, 38 West Fifth Street, Dayton, Ohio 45402. (Professionally made B&W photos for use with variety of current subjects.)

Posters

ARGUS COMMUNICATIONS, 7440 North Natchez Avenue, Niles, Ill. 60648.

ABBEY PRESS, St. Meinrad, Ind. 47577.

Multimedia Materials

PAULIST PRESS, 400 Sette Drive, Paramus, N.J. 07652. (Especially for their "Discovery" series materials.)

FRANCISCAN COMMUNICATIONS CENTER, 1229 South Santee Street, Los Angeles, Calif. 90015.

Printed Materials

UNITED CHURCH OF CHRIST, 287 Park Avenue South, New York, N.Y. 10010.

PAULIST PRESS, 400 Sette Drive, Paramus, N.J. 07652. (Producers of unusually fine printed resources on a wide variety of current issues.)